The Dixon Valley
Its First 250 Years

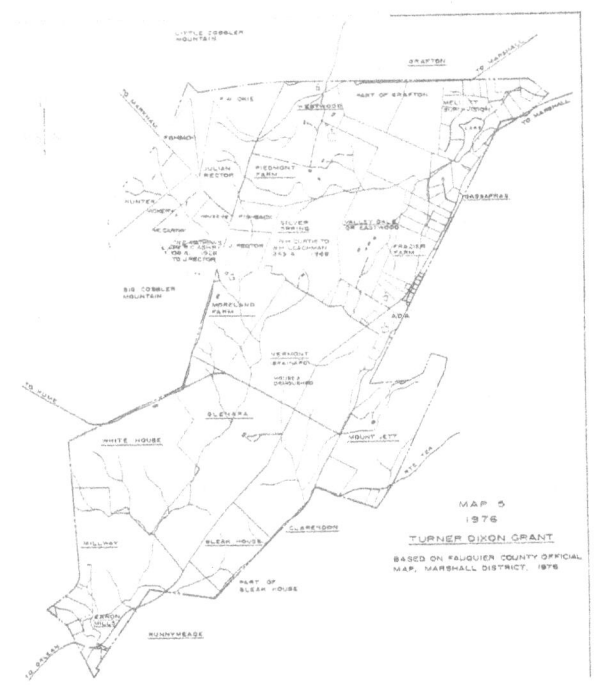

By T. Triplett Russell & John K. Gott

HERITAGE BOOKS
2008

HERITAGE BOOKS
AN IMPRINT OF HERITAGE BOOKS, INC.

Books, CDs, and more—Worldwide

For our listing of thousands of titles see our website at

www.HeritageBooks.com

Published 2008 by
HERITAGE BOOKS, INC.
Publishing Division
100 Railroad Ave. #104
Westminster, Maryland 21157

Copyright © 1991 T. Triplett Russell and John K. Gott

Other books by T. Triplett Russell and John K. Gott:

An Historical Vignette of Oak Hill, Fauquier County: Home of John Marshall, Chief Justice of the United States and Native Son of Fauquier County
Fauquier County in the Revolution
The Dixon Valley, Its First 250 Years

All rights reserved. No part of this book may be reproduced or transmitted in any form or by any means, electronic or mechanical, including photocopying, recording or by any information storage and retrieval system without written permission from the author, except for the inclusion of brief quotations in a review.

International Standard Book Numbers
Paperbound: 978-1-55613-427-2
Clothbound: 978-0-7884-7008-0

Contents

Acknowledgments v

The Maps vii

Introduction ix

1. The Northern Neck Grant 1

2. *Vermont*, 1810–1839 21

3. *Vermont*, 1839–1978 47

Appendix A: Turner Dixon Grant Maps, 1823–1976 127

Appendix B: Life at *Vermont*, 1810–1821 135

Appendix C: The Death of T. Clay Maddux 137

Appendix D: Eastwood/Brown Farm/Valley Dale Farm "Old Stone Chimney" by Barbara B. Searles 143

Appendix E: Slaves of Turner Dixon 147

Index 151

Acknowledgments

The successful writing of local history is dependent on exploring every source available. The court records of Fauquier County are the most complete of any county in Virginia; the arrangement and indexing never fail to make the use of them a delight. This is enhanced by the graciousness of the staff charged with the care of the records.

Personal contact is most important too--without the help of so many this study would have been impossible. We are especially indebted to the late Raymond H. Lee and his sister, Mrs. Lucy Lee Rollins of Falls Church; Mrs. Barbara (Brown) Searles and her father, the late Charles H. Brown, of McLean; Mrs. Alice Fitzhugh Horner Donovan of Great Falls; Mrs. Mary Winston Nelson Fisher of California; Mrs. Elizabeth W. Lindley of Williamsburg; the late Philip Nelson of Warrenton; the late Mrs. Arthur Prettyman of Washington, D. C.; Mrs. Beatrice Ford of Marshall; the late Mrs. Nannie H. Curtis and William F. Curtis of Marshall; Mrs. Arey L. Daniel of Louisiana; Mr. and Mrs. Victor Hacker of Marshall; Mason F. Lunceford, who halted work in the fields of *Mt. Jett* to share his hospitality; the late James H. Davis of Baltimore. To the Hon. J. Page Turner, former mayor of The Plains, Va., teacher and genealogist of the Turner family of King George and Fauquier counties, a special thanks. He spent many hours sharing his expertise on the family; reading the manuscript and offering wise counsel.

At the beginning of this history we had the interest and help of the following indispensable sources of Northern Neck people and places; unfortunately, we cannot share with them the finished product: John A. C. Keith, George H. S. King, Wallace W. Phillips, Mr. and Mrs. George R. Thompson--they were an inspiration.

The maps were produced by the capable hands of Ms. Phyllis A. Hammond of Miami--any faults are the authors'.

The Maps

The maps accompanying this study of the Dixon Valley (Appendix A) are intended to demonstrate that land divisions made over one hundred and fifty years ago had a marked influence on all subsequent land development, and a high percentage of the boundary lines established at that time exist today. It has obviously been impossible in these maps to reflect every minor boundary adjustment or land trade to facilitate the construction of roads, millraces, or other man-made amenities. Minor subdivision of property is also largely ignored.

After the demolition of *Vermont* the oldest structures remaining on the Turner Dixon grant are probably the "Lower House" at *Eastwood* and part of *Westwood*. Both appear to be well cared for and are probably good for a great many more years. Of a little less antiquity but certainly all well over one hundred years old are the *White House*, *Vernon Mills*, and the main house at *Silver Spring*. All are well worth preserving, and the last named, shorn of unfortunate additions, would be an interesting subject for restoration.

From an architectural point of view, certainly the most interesting is *Bleak House*, now in a dilapidated condition and threatened with collapse. It remains from a period that is now attracting the attention of those interested in restoration and has many characteristic features that would make such an attempt both exciting and rewarding. It is to be hoped that someone with the taste and means to accomplish this will come along before the whole thing crumbles to dust.

Introduction

Heroes are creatures of myth. We have read much of the valor of Achilles, but there is a lingering doubt in our minds whether he was a living person or existed only in the mind of the poet. On the other hand, Phocus of Halae was no myth. He may never have performed a valiant deed in his life, but he lived and died. We know because, on the fifteenth of April in the year 431 B.C., he bought one quarter hectare of land near Brauron, twenty miles east of Athens. He is part of recorded history.

So is Charles Burgess. It would never have occurred to him as he left his plantation *Monaskon* on the banks of the Rappahannock River on June 15, 1731, that he was about to perform a deed that would bring his name to our attention nearly 250 years later, after his bones were dust and even his tombstone had long since disappeared. He was a pragmatic man, who was thinking of the future of his family after his death, but his place in history was of little concern to him. Nevertheless, the basic source of history is found in man's innate desire to prove and record his ownership of land so that it may be passed on to his children and his children's children. It is the reason for birth, marriage, and death records, and for wills and deeds. It is from such records that we know nearly all we do know of our forefathers.

So Charles Burgess began his brief odyssey.

1

The Northern Neck Grant

As the skiff rounded Towle's Point and broke out into the broad estuary of Carter's Creek, he could see *Corotoman*, the home of Robert Carter. From the river it looked less like a private manor house than a seaport town stretching along the bank of the creek. Within the breakwater that Carter had built were dozens of large and small craft, including two schooners from England engaged in unloading their cargo of manufactured goods and loading the hogsheads of tobacco that lined the wharf. One of the schooners was the "Carter," in which Carter himself had an interest. The other, Charles Burgess guessed, probably belonged to William Dawkins, Carter's London factor.

The wharf, warehouses, and the sloop landing house were hives of activity. Goods and stores were in constant transit: they were loaded on ox-carts for distribution to the inland or "forest" plantations along the King's Highway as far as the newly created County of Prince William and on sloops for transshipment to Falmouth or Fredericksburg or to one of the many private landings along the Potomac.

The sights, sounds, and smells of the busy dockside assailed the senses of any visitor, but Charles Burgess was oblivious to it all. He did not hear the thunder of tobacco hogsheads rolling across plank decking and the hoarse commands of the ships' officers and Carter's overseers. Even the beauty of the densely forested river bank and the distant prospect of the sea sparkling in the sunlight of that mild June day in 1731 did not move him. He had come on an important mission that could no longer be postponed. And the man he must see was "King" Carter himself.

As he drew closer, the huge, unbeautiful Carter mansion loomed before him, but little removed from the hurly-burly of the dockside. That was the way Carter wanted it--let his children build their stately mansions, *Rosewell*, *Shirley*, or *Carter's Grove*, set on spacious lawns with broad terraces descending to the river. He liked to be in the midst of things, where he could keep an eye on the rambunctious crews of ships and on his own black dockhands, ever ready for a short nap if not watched.

The house itself was not so much a mansion as a cluster of heterogeneous structures, old and new, solid and dilapidated, high and low. Part of it dated from seventy years earlier when Robert Carter's father had settled in Lancaster County. That was the "Old House," now used mainly as a dining room after the fire of 1729. The "New House" was a plain brick structure with little to recommend it but size. It had been built between 1705 and 1710, before there were designers in Virginia skillful enough to create in the fashionable Georgian manner. Carter did not care. Between and around the two main structures he built many undated wings, ells and smaller buildings. These additions housed the kitchens, dairies (old and new), the spinning house, smithy, distillery, and served a dozen other functions as well. There was an old coach house and a new one to shelter Carter's fine new chariot as well as the old coach. There was also an immense brick store. Down by the boatyard were other storehouses for building material. One contained only nails.

Under many of these buildings were cellars containing spirits, including rum and Carter's large store of old wine. When part of this conglomeration of buildings caught fire on a windy night in late January or early February of 1729, the *Maryland Gazette* reported the loss as "very great," but Carter bemoaned only the loss of the larger part of his wine cellar. Charles Burgess knew all of these things. He had served in the House of Burgesses when Carter was President of the Council and had often waited on the imperious "King" with whom he had shared some of that wine. It was always excellent.

Drawing up to the dockside, Burgess left his boatman to tie up the skiff and made straight for the "office." Here, unless Carter was sick abed, he knew he would find him acting in his capacity as Virginia agent for Thomas, Lord Fairfax, Proprietor of the Northern Neck. Once at the office, Burgess could see others had the same idea, and he would have to wait his turn. It was by then all too apparent to land speculators interested in Northern Neck that Robert Carter, at sixty-eight, could not be expected to live much longer. Keeping the land intact for Lord Fairfax had not been easy for Carter. He had fought a stout battle with Virginia's governors (first Spotswood and then Gooch) to preserve the proprietary, with little help from his Lordship. Of late the pressure to fix a western boundary had become stronger. Most settlers felt that it should stop at the "Blew Ridge" and at Hedgman's River, considered the headspring of the Rappahannock.

Carter contended differently. The terms of the latest patent under James II, dated 27 September 1688, clearly stated that the proprietary extended to a line between the "first heads or springs" of the Potomac and Rappahannock. Everyone knew that the headspring of the Potomac was a long way off and that the Rapidan and its tributary, the Conway, was much longer than Hedgman's River.

At stake were, among other things, the vast fertile valley of the Shenandoah, the present Culpeper and Rappahannock counties, and much of Madison County. Patiently and constantly Carter had entered caveats against the grants of the Royal Governor in these areas. It was a matter, though, for the King in Council to decide, and Lord Fairfax had shown little interest in laying it before the Privy Council. In fact, he was not on the best of terms with His Majesty or, especially, His Majesty's prime minister, Robert Walpole.

Furthermore, it was no secret that the lease Carter had made with his Lordship in 1722 was about to expire. Under the lease, Carter had undertaken to pay the Fairfax estate Ŀ450 annually, and he worried about getting new settlers and collecting quit-rents.[1] In 1722, Ŀ450 steady income seemed like quite a lot to Lord Fairfax. In 1731 he was not so sure. In September the lease would expire. What then? The tobacco market was down. Carter was getting old and tired of accommodating his indifferent Lordship. None of Carter's sons showed much interest in carrying on the affairs of the Fairfax proprietorship. Carter was rich beyond dream of avarice--mostly at Fairfax's expense--but there was no certainty that the lease would be renewed at any figure.

So it seemed to Colonel Charles Burgess of St. Mary's White Chapel that it was high time to secure for himself and his descendants some of the choice land that might soon be beyond his grasp. As a member of the House of Burgesses, [2] he had gotten on well with Carter and knew that Governor Gooch, for all his mild exterior, would negotiate shrewdly. If the outcome of the dispute over the boundary was in doubt, it would be well if his Fairfax grant was east of the Blue Ridge and Hedgman's River. He knew also that it would be unwise to procrastinate. John Warner's surveys were being patented almost as fast as he could make them.

As Charles Burgess moved through the throng outside the estate office, he recognized many of his friends and neighbors bent on the same mission. Among them was Major James Ball of *Bewdley*. Burgess's mother-in-law had been Hannah Ball, sister of Captain William Ball of *Millenbeck*, a wealthy planter in Lancaster County.³ Captain Ball was dead, but his son, Major James Ball, was a first cousin of Burgess's wife.

Possibly Major Ball had inspired Burgess to this sudden desire for vast tracts of wilderness land, to which Ball was also heavily committed. Otherwise, it is difficult to understand Burgess's need for it. He had no sons, only three daughters between five and eight years old. His family in England consisted of four spinster sisters, who were, according to Hayden, "poor as Job."⁴ Their unenviable condition was owing no doubt to lack of a dowry. Possibly Burgess was determined that his three small daughters would never have to face such a consequence.

The estate office, but loosely attached to the Mansion House, was, like it, on the inside a confused jumble of new and old furniture, odd pieces of bric-a-brac, and miscellaneous odds and ends. Books and papers were everywhere--on tables, chairs, and sometimes on the floor. Only Carter knew where things were, and he, not always. The room was hot. The old man sat in a chair by the fireplace in which a fire burned. Even on this pleasantly warm June day, the old man was cold. He glanced through Burgess's patents without comment. They seemed in order.

It is possible, though unlikely, that Burgess had seen the land he had come to claim. In 1732 the area was virtually uninhabited, covered with towering forests, without roads, and with scarcely any paths to follow. Landmarks were almost non-existent, but John Warner, the surveyor, knew his way around. On his master map of the Fairfax Proprietary, begun in 1736, only one landmark in what is now Fauquier County is shown, that of "Cobler Mount ^{N}." This lonely hill, which seems to stand apart and tower over its neighbors, was already referred to as "The Big Cobler." At the foot of this rock pile was very choice land, and quite a large piece of it had been surveyed for Burgess.

So it happened that, on 15 June 1731, Robert Carter signed patents for Charles Burgess totaling the incredible sum of 20,155 acres of land in Prince William County, an area which, twenty-eight years later, would be Fauquier.

The land was in three tracts as follows:

1. 13,879 acres on the east side of Goose Creek and extending to "Crummy's" [Crommell's] Run (N. N. G. Bk. C, p. 162).

2. 3,230 acres at the south end of the mountains known as Coblers, near a branch of Carter's Run (N.N.G. Bk. C, p. 163).

3. 3,046 acres at the mouth of a small branch of Rappahannock River and the Main North Run thereof (N.N.G. Bk. C, p. 164).

Even that was not enough. Two days later Burgess was back in Carter's office securing 1,176 acres on the east side of Goose Creek and at the foot of North Cobler's Mountain (N.N.G. Bk. C, p. 167).

The first of these grants, the one for 13,879 acres, was apparently intended by Burgess to be a permanent landed estate to descend to his grandchildren. The rest was more or less speculative. In any event, the first tract was not listed among the assets of the estate of Charles Burgess addressed to His Majesty by Burgess's heirs after his death in 1733.[5]

Shortly after his second visit to "King" Carter, Burgess began to reflect that he had unwisely put all his eggs in one basket. If the outcome of the dispute with Governor Gooch should come out as Burgess expected it might, what was to stop the Privy Council from nullifying all of the Proprietary grants under Carter's lease? There was widespread dissatisfaction with the Carter management even on the part of the Lord Proprietor. Immense tracts had been granted by Carter to his children and grandchildren, some so young that they could not legally execute leases. The situation did not encourage settlement, in fact quite the contrary. Burgess decided that it was a good idea to hedge his bets.

His Prince William County land at the foot of the Big Cobler totaled (excluding his first 13,879 acres) 7,452 acres. He promptly applied for a like amount, 7,400 acres in Spotsylvania County in the "Great Fork of Rappahannock" (now Culpeper County). The governor took some risk in granting this patent because it had been generally agreed that no patents were to be granted in the disputed area until action was taken by the Privy Council.

However, Carter himself had set a dangerous precedent. Before Gooch's arrival in Virginia, Carter, as President of the Council and acting governor, had granted 2,000 acres in the Little Fork of the Rappahannock (above Thornton's Run) to Henry Willis of Fredericksburg.

The grant had raised a storm of protest at the time, and the wily Willis had palmed it off on a defenseless widow in exchange for more legitimate land patents in Gloucester County. By this act, Carter had tacitly admitted that Hedgman's River formed a boundary of the Proprietary, so the governor doubtless felt that he was justified in granting Burgess his patent.

On September 13, 1731, when Carter's lease had only a few more days to run, Burgess made his last journey to *Corotoman* to obtain a land patent. This was for 2,925 acres in Prince William County "on ye side of a mountain between two small vallies near the head of Goose Creek." This raised the total of his acres in what would later be Fauquier County to 24,256.

He was lucky. It was just in the nick of time. Some waited too long. The expiration date of the lease passed without anything happening, and Carter continued as before. Charles Taylor of Prince William County obtained a grant for 1,700 acres adjoining Major James Ball, dated 9 May 1732. Three days later Robert Carter wrote his friend William Dawkins in London, "Tomorrow morning, God willing, I am setting out on the doleful occasion of my dear son Robert's funeral ... it has pleased the Almighty to take [him] from me in the flower of his age, to my great grief and confusion...." Robert, nicknamed Robin, had been his second son. John, the eldest, would inherit much of his estate, but Robin was his favorite, the one most likely to have carried on his business as he wanted it. Robin left his wife, Priscilla, a daughter and a four-year-old son named Robert.

For "King" Carter life held little more. All the rest was downhill. On the fourth of August Carter was dead. No specific cause is given--possibly it was just grief and old age. Charles Taylor's patent was left unsigned and, according to a later record in the patent book, "so stands for nothing."[6]

In death, Charles Burgess was soon to follow Robert Carter. Again, the cause is unknown. We do not have the date of his birth, but he cannot have been very old. He married Frances Fox in 1721, and his three daughters were still children. However, less than three months after Carter's funeral, on 4 November 1732, he wrote his will. Possibly he did not finish it. He mentions his wife and his four sisters in England, but he gives no instructions concerning the future of his immense landed estate in the Northern Neck and elsewhere, 31,656 acres in all. On 14 March 1733 his will was recorded in the Lancaster County Court by his executors, his wife, Major Joseph Ball, and his friend Edwin Conway, brother of Major Ball's deceased wife.[7]

The provisions (or lack of them) in Burgess's will left his widow, Frances, in a rather awkward position. His executors could not sell the land or the large number of slaves; and his personal estate consisted "mostly of outstanding debts, many of which are precarious or cannot be recovered in any short time." Against them were "many great debts ... which exceed and must exhaust the whole value of the said slaves and personal estate."

The executors had, therefore, no recourse but to ask "his most excellent Majesty" for authority to sell the land "at the best price that can be got, all, or any part of the said seventeen thousand, seven hundred and seventy-seven acres of land ... and the money ... applied in the first place to pay the debts, and then the legacies of the said Charles Burges."[8]

Significantly, there was no mention of the 13,879 acres patented on Goose Creek in the northeast corner of what is now Fauquier County. That would be the patrimony of his grandsons, Burgess Ball and Burgess Smith. They did not keep the property, but that was their fault, not his.

Not long afterwards, Frances (Fox) Burgess married Jesse Ball, eldest son of Major James Ball; and, in the goodness of time, two of her daughters, Margaret and Elizabeth Burgess, married two of Jesse Ball's younger brothers, James, Jr., and Jeduthon. Thus came about a Virginia genealogical tangle that has baffled students for well over two hundred years. The Ball interests in Fauquier persisted for many years after the creation of the county in 1759, but the Burgess land belonged to others.[9]

After the death of Robert Carter, Lord Fairfax apparently quickly realized that if he hoped to have any income from his Virginia estates he must tend to them himself. He halted the issuance of Proprietary grants until the Privy Council could take up the thorny question of his boundary dispute with the Virginia colony.

Accordingly, on 29 November 1733 the Privy Council placed in his hands an order directing the lieutenant governor of the Virginia colony to appoint commissioners to find out just where the headsprings of the Potomac and Rappahannock Rivers really were. Meanwhile, the Lieutenant Governor was not to "presume to make" any patents in the disputed area. In February 1735 Lord Fairfax, probably with some distaste, "kiss'd His Majesty's hand, being ready to set out for his Proprietary in Virginia." Fairfax had little use for the fat German whose round posterior occupied the English throne. As far as the King was concerned, his Lordship's Virginia estates may as well have been on the moon.

After some delay and an uncomfortable sea voyage that lasted weeks, Lord Fairfax arrived in Virginia in May of 1735. It was then that he realized how vast his Virginia estates were, how incredibly valuable. He visited Fauquier County and pushed farther into what would one day be his home in the valley of the Shenandoah. Everything delighted him except the state of Carter's books. He was "disappointed by the irregularity of the books ... for I have not yet been able to get from them a list of all the land they hold, some whereof is not to be found in the books and none of it in the rent rolls."[10]

Another thing that troubled him was that the land surveyors, among them John Warner for King George County, William Ball for Lancaster and Northumberland, Captain Barber for Richmond, and one other surveyor, expressed doubts as to the true extent of the Proprietary and the propriety of surveying land until the boundary suit was settled. Fairfax agreed and knew that he must return to England to accomplish that end. After a relatively brief stay in Virginia he returned to England.

The Commission report made on 27 July 1739 was favorable to the Fairfax interests but, as long as Walpole was Prime Minister, the boundary case dragged. Finally, in 1742, Walpole ran into trouble and was forced to resign. His successor was the Duke of Newcastle, a friend of Lord Fairfax. Under the Duke's prodding, the Privy Council was moved to act in Fairfax's favor. On 11 April 1745, the boundary dispute was settled with one important proviso. Lord Fairfax undertook to honor all of the patents that had been granted by the Virginia governors within the bounds of the Proprietary since its beginning. Fairfax readily acquiesced. There was plenty of land left and no useful purpose would be served by incurring the wrath of those who had occupied land under the aegis of the Royal Governor. While Lord Fairfax was back in England, the affairs of the Proprietary were handled by his cousin, William Fairfax, imported from Massachusetts for the purpose. William Fairfax rented a "good and convenient house ... well situated for the King's business and the Proprietor's," on the ridge between Westmoreland and King George Counties. However, for the most part, he played a waiting game.

However, he did one thing of interest. On 18 November 1740, he re-granted the land surveyed by John Warner for Charles Taylor in 1732.[11] Taylor was dead by then and the unsigned grant was worthless to his heirs. The new grantee was Harry Turner of King George County, Virginia. The grant was for 1,700 acres, roughly 980 feet square with one corner lopped off. It was "at the North Cobler Mountain and joyning to the land surveyed for Capt. James Ball ... and John Blowers and extending ... across a branch of Goose Creek."[12]

Thus the youthful Harry Turner steps upon the stage of recorded history as the first of his name who probably intended one day to live at the foot of the Big Cobbler. He was the eldest son of Colonel Thomas Turner, sometime member of the

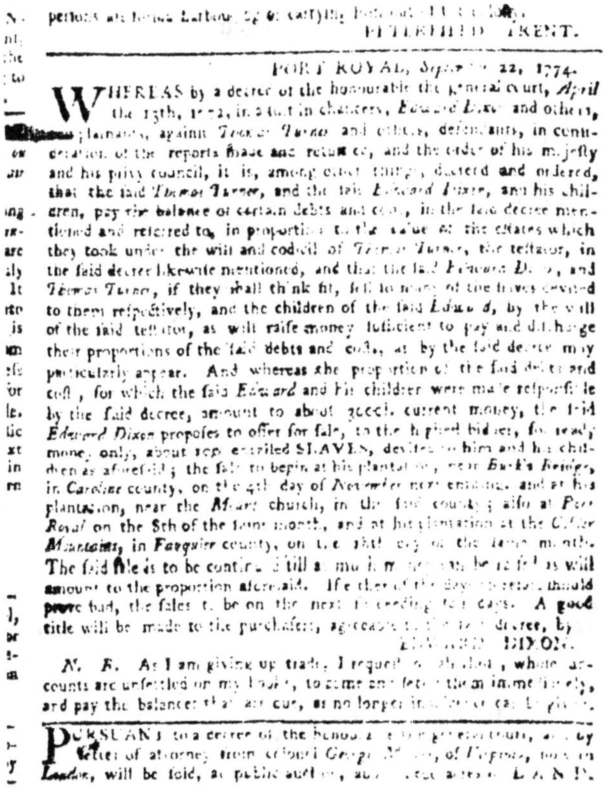

persons are forbid harbouring or carrying him out of the colony.
PETERFIELD TRENT.

PORT ROYAL, September 22, 1774.

WHEREAS by a decree of the honourable the general court, *April* the 13th, 1772, in a suit in chancery, *Edward Dixon* and others, complainants, against *Thomas Turner* and others, defendants, in consideration of the reports made and returned, and the order of his majesty and his privy council, it is, among other things, decreed and ordered, that the said *Thomas Turner*, and the said *Edward Dixon*, and his children, pay the balance of certain debts and costs, in the said decree mentioned and referred to, in proportion to the value of the estates which they took under the will and codicil of *Thomas Turner*, the testator, in the said decree likewise mentioned, and that the said *Edward Dixon*, and *Thomas Turner*, if they shall think fit, sell so many of the slaves devised to them respectively, and the children of the said *Edward*, by the will of the said testator, as will raise money sufficient to pay and discharge their proportions of the said debts and costs, as by the said decree may particularly appear. And whereas the proportion of the said debts and costs, for which the said *Edward* and his children were made responsible by the said decree, amount to about 900l. current money, the said *Edward Dixon* proposes to offer for sale, to the highest bidder, for ready money only, about 100 entailed SLAVES, devised to him and his children as aforesaid; the sale to begin at his plantation, near *Buck's Bridge*, in *Caroline* county, on the 4th day of *November* next ensuing, and at his plantation, near the *Mount* church, in the said county; also at *Port Royal* on the 8th of the same month, and at his plantation at the *Cobler Mountains*, in *Fauquier* county, on the 18th day of the same month. The said sale is to be continued till as much money is raised as will amount to the proportion aforesaid. If either of the days appointed should prove bad, the sales to be on the next succeeding fair days. A good title will be made to the purchasers, agreeable to the said decree, by

EDWARD DIXON.

N. B. As I am giving up trade, I request of all those, whose accounts are unsettled on my books, to come and settle them immediately, and pay the balances that are due, as no longer indulgence can be given.

PURSUANT to a decree of the honourable the general court, and by letter of attorney from colonel *George Mason*, of *Virginia*, now in *London*, will be sold, at public auction, about [illegible] acres of LAND,

An advertisement from the *Virginia Gazette*, Williamsburg, Va., by Edward Dixon (ca. 1702–1779) who had married Sarah Turner, the daughter of Thomas Turner (d: 1758) of King George County. Capt. Edward Dixon had established a "quarter" (usually meant having slaves on the land supervised by an overseer) in the Dixon's Valley by 1774. The tract "at his plantation at the Cobler Mountains" had been devised to Capt. Dixon's son, Turner, by his grandfather Turner. Turner Dixon (ca. 1751–1785) never married and the property descended to his brother, Harry Dixon, and to his son, John Edward Henry Turner Dixon (1780–1820), known simply as Turner Dixon.

House of Burgesses from King George County, and his first wife, Martha Taliaferro. In 1740 Harry was about twenty-five. Three years later he married Elizabeth Smith, only daughter and heiress of Colonel Nicholas Smith of *Smith Mount* near Leedstown, then in King George County (now Westmoreland). With probably no thought of moving into the wilds of Fauquier, he lived at the time on his wife's inherited estate. There, in 1745, his son Thomas was born. His wife died in 1750, probably in an attempt to give him another child.

Harry Turner lost no time in finding another to care for his motherless boy. In 1751 he married 15-year-old Elizabeth Fauntleroy, daughter of Colonel William Fauntleroy of Richmond County. However, before the year was out he suddenly died of causes that have never been explained. In his will he left almost his entire estate to his infant son, Thomas Turner. He gave custody of the boy to his "Honoured Father" and also gave him the management of his estate.

For Colonel Thomas Turner the 1,700 acres represented but a few more to add to the thousands of acres he already managed throughout the Northern Neck. He had one other son, Thomas, by his first wife, Martha Taliaferro, and two daughters by his second wife, sister to the first. They were Mary, who apparently never married, and Sarah who, in 1748, had married Captain Edward Dixon, an extremely well-to-do storekeeper in Port Royal, Caroline County. Edward and Sarah (Turner) Dixon had, in 1751, a two-year-old son, Harry Dixon. By a sad chain of circumstances, Sarah Dixon, too, apparently died giving birth to a second son, Turner Dixon. Her death and that of her brother Harry Turner came within a few months of each other.[13]

It was probably during the ensuing seven years that Colonel Turner picked up one of the Burgess grants close to his Cobbler Mountain tract. As we have seen, the Burgess grants had been for sale since 1735, but it is unlikely that the canny Turner would have invested in them until after the Fairfax case was settled in 1745. This tract was one of those Charles Burgess had patented on 15 June 1731. It was for 3,230 acres in what was then the County of Prince William, "beginning at the pile of stone ... at the south end of the Mountains known by the name of Coblers ... running to a large Spanish oak on the East side of a Branch of the Rappahannock [Thumb Run], etc." It also touched a branch of Carter's Run and ran along Blower's line. He probably bought it sight unseen. More than sixty years were to pass before anyone took a really close look at it.[14]

Colonel Thomas Turner died in 1758. His estate was divided among his three grandsons, Thomas Turner, 13, Harry

Dixon, 9, and Turner Dixon, 7. To the last he left his tract at the foot of the Big Cobbler, said at the time to contain "upwards of 3,000 acres."[15]

The boy's father, Captain Edward Dixon, ca. 1702-1779, was looking out for his son's interest with vigilant determination to increase his inheritance. He had the Burgess grant re-surveyed and, along with it, a grant to Lewis Ellzey made only two and a half months after the original Burgess grant, and abutting it to the north. Additional to this was a large area of waste and ungranted land west of the Ellzey patent.

North of Ellzey's patent was one thousand acres originally granted to John Blowers and, in March 1730, re-granted to John Mercer, who sold it to Colonel Thomas Harrison. Apparently Ellzey had also defaulted on his patent, so the whole area was up for grabs. Edward Dixon and Thomas Harrison decided to split this tract. The Harrison moiety became part of *Grafton*. Dixon's moiety was simply added to the north end of the Burgess patent, making a total of 4,406 acres. Captain Dixon obtained a new grant, dated 11 June 1777, for the full amount during his lifetime, and after his death, to go to his son Turner Dixon. Captain Dixon died two years later, when the heir was twenty-eight.

Turner Dixon certainly had little interest in the 4,406 acres of land in the remote wilderness, which had, since 1759, fallen into the new county of Fauquier. He had plenty of land elsewhere: 843 acres in Caroline County, 368 acres on Deep Run,[16] more than a 1,000 acres in Fairfax County. As he grew older, he followed a course that was at once typical of the young scions of wealth and remarkably hard on those who were interested in protecting their estates. He liked high living, and it is extremely doubtful that he even visited his remote acres, unless hunting appealed to him. The land abounded in game. Gambling seems to have been the outlet for his high spirits. In 1773 when the Committee of Safety grew suddenly puritanical and attempted to cut off all "frivolity," Captain Turner Dixon was charged with gambling at a tavern in Port Royal.[17] About the same time he undertook the raising of a company of militia in Caroline County. His subsequent participation in the Revolutionary War is less easily substantiated. He had no children and died in 1785 at the age of thirty-four. He left his Cobbler Mountain tract to the five-year-old son of his older brother, Harry.

Although what we know of the life of Harry Dixon is considerably more decorous than that of his younger brother, it did not serve to prolong his years. At age thirty he married Alice Fitzhugh, daughter of John and Alice (Thornton) Fitzhugh of *Bellaire*, Stafford County. Their only son, John Edward Henry Turner Dixon, was the heir to his uncle's land in Fauquier. He was born in 1780, and was followed a year later by his sister, Elizabeth Dixon. When he was three years old, his father died and his mother almost immediately married John Birkett Pratt of *Camden*, Caroline County, a man two years her junior. In addition to his two stepchildren, John Pratt soon had two of his own, Alice Fitzhugh, born in 1785, and John Birkett Pratt, Jr., born in 1789.

The child with all the names (called simply Turner Dixon), as sole heir of both his father and uncle who themselves had inherited substantial estates from their father and grandfather, was fortunate in having a stepfather who concerned himself with improving rather than wasting his inheritance. It was under the direction of John Pratt that the development of the Fauquier County land was well begun. He established an overseer on the property with enough Negroes to clear land and plant crops.[18] We may be sure that the men sent to this Siberia were not the most easily managed. That fact became evident in 1793.

On 29 January 1793, Charles Marshall, gentleman, attorney for the Commonwealth for the County of Fauquier, informed the Fauquier County Court that "Daniel, a negro man, slave, the property of Turner Dixon's estate, not having God before his eyes, but being moved and seduced by the Instigation of the Devil did ... with force and arms ... entered in and upon one Rhody Cave, daughter of Thomas Cave, who is an infant under the age of Ten years, in the peace of God ... then and there being, violently and feloniously did make an Assault on her ... against the will of her, the said Rhody Cave, then and there feloniously did ravish and carnally know, against the peace of the Commonwealth and against the forms of the laws in that case made and provided." Found guilty, and having nothing to say for himself except that he was innocent, Daniel was hanged. The Court placed a value on him of L40.[19]

The Dixon Negroes were apparently a continuing source of trouble. Some were received into the Baptist Church on Thumb Run in 1798 and 1799, but, of them, some were promptly excommunicated. One Negro Morten, the property of Turner "Dickson," was ousted for "grose immorality, Viz: Fornacion and Obstinial imperantincy, &c." The latter, it appears, was a particularly heinous crime. "Brothers" Morehead and Holmes, neighbors, were asked to look into the matter of the conduct of the Dixon Negroes in 1803 and make a report. Presumably, it was not favorable as far as one Sylvie was concerned. One month later she was "excluded from us." Events were shaping themselves, however, that would put an end to the "grose immorality," on the Dixon lands.[20]

Early in 1800 Turner Dixon was keeping bachelor hall in Caroline County, where he had twenty Negroes (not counting children under twelve) and eight horses. However, before the year was out, "on Sunday the 9th of November," he changed all that.[21] He married his fifteen-year-old second cousin, Maria Turner, daughter of Colonel Thomas and Jane (Fauntleroy) Turner of Richmond County. Quite probably on a gray November day a merry throng attended the wedding of the young Dixon heir, not yet twenty-one, and his child bride at *Walsingham*, the Turner home opposite Port Royal. Neither the tender age of the couple nor their consanguinity was unusual, but the result was tragedy that would play itself out in the distant hills of Fauquier.

The young Dixons were still contemplating living in the tidewater in June of 1802, more than a year after their marriage. At that time Dixon bought land in Essex County from Thomas Lomax. To secure the necessary funds, he gave his stepfather, John Pratt, a mortgage on his Cobbler Mountain land. What had been called in his uncle's will "upwards of 3,000 acres," is called in the mortgage to John Pratt dated 4 June 1802, "all that tract ... in the County of Fauquier near the Cobler Mountain belonging to the said Turner Dixon containing about 4,500 acres." What had happened in the meanwhile? [22]

In fact, the tract in question never did contain 4,500 acres, but it did contain a great many more than 3,000. One wonders if young Dixon knew this, or was just guessing. As far as is known no survey had then been made. Perhaps he had learned from surveys of adjacent land that there was more in the Burgess survey than had been expected. Perhaps he had additional land nearby that he included in the mortgage, though the fact is not mentioned. It is useless to speculate and it made no difference to John Pratt. It was only security for a loan and its exact size did not matter.

Turner and Maria Dixon had their first child only ten months after their marriage, daughter Elizabeth Matilda, born 21 September 1801. She was followed every year or so, with machine-like regularity, by other offspring, for a total of eleven more children. Before she was thirty-three, Maria Dixon had twelve children. Preposterous as it may seem today, such a record was by no means uncommon. Miraculously, in this instance, all survived to maturity.

The Dixons were still in Essex County when their second child, Henry Thomas Dixon, was born, 28 July 1803. In

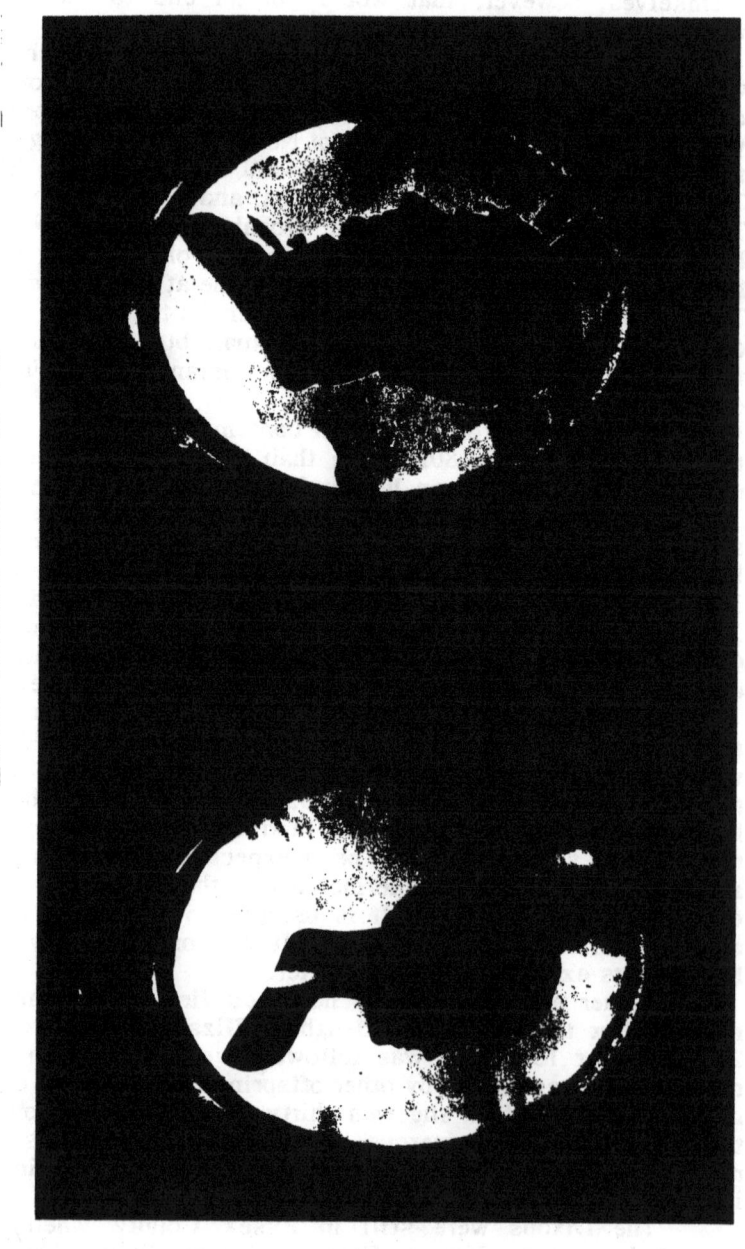

Turner Dixon (1780-1821) and Maria (Turner) Dixon (1785-1847) of *Vermont*
--courtesy of Professor H. M. Dixon

Maria (Turner) Dixon
1745-1847
Wife of Turner Dixon, Esq., of *Vermont*

--courtesy of Mrs. Mary W. N. Fisher

Henry Thomas Dixon (1803-1865)
son of Turner and Maria (Turner) Dixon

--courtesy of Cynthia Hvisdock Preloh

a letter dated 19 October of that year, the young Hugh Mercer, son of the Revolutionary War hero, wrote to his friend Gabriel Lewis in Lexington, Kentucky, "Our races are just over. Our town was more crowded with company that attended them than I have ever known it. Col. Selden of Richmond, Col. Hoomes and Turner Dixon won the Purses, which were considerable."[23] It is unlikely that Dixon brought horses down from Fauquier at that time, to race at Fredericksburg. In fact, it is not certain just when he reached a decision to move his family to Fauquier. That move was probably made sometime between 8 April 1805, the birth date of his second daughter, Mary Jane, and 10 October 1810, the day on which his satisfaction of the mortgage on his Fauquier land, given to his stepfather in 1802, was recorded.

It is not known exactly what buildings were on the land in 1810. There was a requirement for "seating" the Fairfax lands with a house sixteen feet square, but that requirement was not always met. There must have been an overseer's house and slave quarters, as we have documentary evidence that slaves were quartered there. There was also a blacksmith's shop which must have existed since at least 1800. In the April Court that year, John Pratt, acting for Turner Dixon, sued George Page for payment for work done at his smithy and won a judgment. There was no "mansion house." That would come later.

The first thing Turner Dixon must turn his attention to was getting an accurate survey of his property. He had the 80-year-old Burgess grant surveyed, giving the metes and bounds of the land, which is easily plotted today. That, however, did not answer his purpose. He got Charles Kemper, Sr., county surveyor of Fauquier County, to make the survey under the watchful eyes of "Gen'l" John Marshall (later Chief Justice of the United States), John Scott, an attorney, son of the Reverend John Scott of Gordonsdale, and himself. This boundary survey, made in 1811, was the basis for the later survey made by Charles Kemper which determined the configuration of the Dixon property as we know it today.

A comparison of this survey with that of the Burgess grant is astonishing. The bearing of every boundary line is identical with the original grant. The distances between the station points, however, in almost all instances, systematically increased. The result is that the Burgess grant, which, accurately computed, did contain 3,230 acres, now contains 4,000 acres. How this came about is hard to say. Neither Marshall nor Scott cared how much land Turner Dixon claimed. The boundaries of Marshall's *Oak Hill* and Scott's *Gordonsdale* had been fixed long since. At whose expense did this expansion take place? One cannot be certain, but if one may hazard a guess, the chief contributor appears to have been John Blower.

In the 1731 Burgess grant, it is stated quite clearly that the north boundary is 685 perches or poles "along the said Blower's his line"; at this point is a single departure from the configuration later established when the boundaries of *Vermont*, were surveyed. Yet in 1821 the northern boundary was *Grafton*, known to have been built on the southern portion of the 1,000-acre patent, dated 1 March 1730, and sold to Colonel Thomas Harrison, 8 July 1765. The answer to this conflicting information is found in the re-grant of Charles Taylor's void patent to Harry Turner in 1740. It reads "Beginning ... three red oaks corner to the lands of said James Ball and the land surveyed for John Blowers near Mr. Mercer's" and ends, "thence binding on the land surveyed for John Blowers, now Mercers." Somehow, in the shifting about of titles, Turner got 770 more acres, and Mercer got the rest. The 1,700-acre Turner (formerly Charles Taylor) grant was sold in 1773 to Colonel Thomas Marshall, father of John Marshall, and became the nucleus of *Oak Hill*.

Having secured his land, Turner Dixon looked about him and saw that it was good. His next order of business was to select a site for his house and build upon it.

Notes for Chapter 1

1. Fairfax Harrison, *Virginia Land Grants*, (Richmond: Old Dominion Press, 1925), p. 161.
2. Fairfax Harrison, *Landmarks of Old Prince William*, (Richmond: Old Dominion Press, 1924), p. 254.
3. H. Ragland Eubank, *The Authentic Guide Book of Historic Northern Neck of Virginia*, (Colonial Beach, Va.: The Northern Neck Association, c1934), p. 93.
4. Horace Edwin Hayden, *Virginia Genealogies*, (Washington, D. C.: A. L. Sauls Planograph Co., 1931) p. 61.
5. William Waller Hening, *The Statutes at Large: Being a Collection of all the Laws of Virqinia ...*, (New York: Bartow, 1823), IV, pp. 451-453.
6. Northern Neck Grants, Book D, p. 90.
7. Hayden, *Virginia Genealogies*, p. 90.
8. Harrison, *Landmarks*, p. 254. Mr. Harrison states that Charles Burgess's "name has a curious interest because, in a suit by his widow, which was appealed from the General Court to the Privy Council, the record showed that in 1736 Mrs. Burgess had somewhere in Virginia [could it have been in Old Prince William?] a tenant named Lemuel Gulliver!! [*Acts of the Privy Council*, Colonial, iii, p. 530]. Dean Swift had heard of this man in England in 1728 and was greatly entertained by a report of 'his ill reputation of being a liar' [see *Correspondence of Jonathan Swift*, ed. Ball, iv, 29]."
9. Eubank, *Historic Northern Neck*, p. 94. Hayden, *Virginia Genealogies*, pp. 60-61.
10. Stuart E. Brown, Jr., *Virginia Baron, The Story of Thomas 6th Lord Fairfax*, (Berryville: Chesapeake Book Co., c1965), p. 58.
11. Northern Neck Grants, Book D, p. 90.
12. Northern Neck Grants, Book E, p. 198.
13. George H. S. King, *Marriaqes of Richmond County, Virginia, 1668-1853*, (Fredericksburg: Author, 1964), p. 266.
14. Northern Neck Grants, Book C, p. 163.

15. *Virginia Magazine of History and Biography*, v. 20, p. 439.
16. ibid.
17. T. E. Campbell, *Colonial Caroline*, (Richmond: 1954), p. 247.
18. The tithable lists refer to the tract as "Dixon's Quarter."
19. *Calendar of Virginia State Papers* ..., (Richmond: By authority of the Legislature, 1875-1893), VI, pp. 272-273.
20. *Thumb Run Baptist Church Minute Books, 1772-1875*, abstracted by John K. Gott, unpublished.
21. George H. S. King, "Dixon - Turner Sampler" in: National Genealogical Society *Quarterly*, Vol. 52, p. 36.
22. Fauquier County Deed Book 15, p. 266.
23. Durrett Papers, Chicago Historical Society.

2

Vermont
1810 - 1839

The land known today as the Dixon Valley was, in the early years of the nineteenth century, an incredibly verdant basin in the foothills of the Blue Ridge Mountains. To the west, alone and majestic, loomed the "Big Cobbler." On the east were hills of lesser height. All were covered from top to bottom with dense forest. In springtime the hills were a vivid green. It took no particular imagination to name the house, on a slight rise facing the mountain, "Vermont."

The Mansion House that Turner Dixon built for his growing family sometime between 1810 and 1815 no longer exists, so it is impossible to give it the careful scrutiny that would be necessary to establish its architectural origins. It was apparently added to an older structure of logs that dated from the end of the previous century. The newer structure was a rectangular, frame country house of simple and pleasing proportions. There was a large, square, central hall with a handsome stair leading to the second floor. The rooms flanking it were also squarish, with good millwork and fine hardware. The fact that the 70-year-old house was thought worth moving to a different site in 1882 is simple testimony to its sturdiness and intrinsic value.[1]

From a single photograph (ca. 1935), we see that a beautifully proportioned Doric portico was added about 1830. On examination it appears probable that it was done by William S. (or H.) Sutton, to whom is attributed more than a dozen Greek Revival houses in the Marshall/Delaplane area. Sutton called himself a carpenter and had no formal architectural training, but he was a marvelous craftsman. He probably worked from a "pattern book," which he followed faithfully. Although it is said that he built some houses, he also added stylish detail to existing houses and probably is responsible for the interior paneling and staircase at *Vermont*. He flourished between 1820 and 1850. The portico at *Glenville* near The Plains (built 1837), may be identical to the one destroyed at *Vermont*.

Though the house was relatively large, its simple plan granted little privacy to the Dixon family as new family members arrived. On 17 March 1806, a second son was born, Turner, and on 13 November 1807, a third, George Beverley. Then came Edward Dixon, born 7 March 1810, and William, born 2 March 1811.

The third daughter, Alice Fitzhugh, was born 25 October 1812. After her came four more sons, John, born 17 April 1814; Charles C., 30 June 1815; Lucius, 10 September 1816; and Alexander, 30 November 1817. After almost continuous pregnancy for seventeen years it would not be surprising if Maria Dixon was exhausted, but she was made of more durable stuff than her husband, who collapsed and died suddenly in March of 1820.

During his life at *Vermont* Turner Dixon made several modest additions to the estate. The first of these was at the extreme south end of the property. At 102 acres, it was not large, but was valuable because it contained a fine mill site on Thumb Run. Dixon purchased the lease of Archibald McClaren from John Marshall on 31 May 1814.[2] Later that year, on the sixteenth of August, he bought another Marshall lease, a narrow strip of land containing 109 acres along his eastern boundary that had been leased to Daniel Flowerree Payne.[3] Both of these leases had been part of the Manor of Leeds and are dutifully recorded on Charles Kemper's great plat of the manor dated 2 July 1815.

Not recorded on that plat was Turner Dixon's third and last additional purchase. William Rust owned 195 3/4 acres paralleling the Payne lease and totaling with it 304 3/4 acres. Dixon bought the Rust land on 4 April 1817.[4] These three tracts together with his original holdings brought the total to 4,407 acres, the amount of land that was divided among his heirs after his death.

That John Marshall was selling land from Leeds Manor instead of leasing it comes as a surprise, as it was against his policy. Marshall was living at Richmond at the time but, in 1818, was building a house at *Oak Hill*, adjoining the original house, for his son Thomas, who had married Margaret Lewis of *Weyanoke*. He may have been a bit short of cash, and Turner Dixon may have happened along at the right time. The latter was at the prime of life and had every reason to expect that many fruitful years lay ahead.[5] Unfortunately, that was not in store for him. Already his days were numbered.

Vermont in its new setting after being removed from the present site of *Glenara* by Benjamin F. Rixey in 1882. Picture taken ca. 1935 when it was the home of Norval Ramey and family. Demolished in 1974. --courtesy Alice Ramey Payne

Vermont mansion as delineated on the 1821 survey of *Vermont* by Charles Kemper, Surveyor of Fauquier County.

--Fauquier County Records Division of Estate of Turner Dixon

Only one of his children was married during his lifetime, his eldest daughter, Elizabeth Matilda, who at the age of seventeen, married Alexander Brown Scott of *Meadow Grove*. The bridegroom was the second son of Alexander Scott (1762-1819) and his first wife, Frances Whiting. On the death of his father the same year, young Scott inherited a property known as *Grenville* (probably *Greenville* on the Shenandoah River in Frederick County). There he took his young bride, but she died in August of 1820, probably in childbirth, six months after her father.

The sudden death of Turner Dixon at the age of forty must have brought considerable consternation to his family. He left no will and his eldest son, Henry Thomas Dixon, was not yet seventeen. Furthermore, as events later proved, the young man was, to say the least, irrational. The responsibility thrown on the youthful Alexander B. Scott, the only male representative of the Dixon family who had reached his majority, was enormous. He seems to have accepted it gracefully, but he soon realized that he had taken on more than he had bargained for. After the death of Scott's wife, the other heirs of Turner Dixon attempted to exclude him from his wife's inheritance. In the long, sometimes disgraceful, history of the Dixon family, Scott was one of few who emerged with his reputation intact.

Major Thomas Turner, Maria Dixon's brother, took charge of the estate, and with the court-appointed commissioners, instructed Charles Kemper, Jr., surveyor, to divide the land into eleven equal parts after subtraction of the dower land. This survey was recorded 24 September 1821, and Alexander B. Scott became painfully aware that the right of his deceased wife had been ignored.[6] He had not, however, been ignored when it came to responsibility for the Dixon children. Almost immediately, 25 April 1820, he found himself guardian of George, aged thirteen and Edward, ten. Although Major Turner assumed guardianship of the six youngest children on 22 May 1820, the following January Alexander B. Scott found himself guardian of two more, Mary Jane, aged sixteen, and Turner, fifteen. At the same time Edward Brooke, Jr., was appointed guardian of Henry Thomas Dixon.[7]

Apparently, Alexander B. Scott protested this turn of events rather vehemently both as to the exclusion from the division of the land and the sudden responsibility for four teenage children. In the latter matter, he obtained results. On the 22 October 1821, Dr. Chandler Peyton, of *Gordonsdale*, a relative of Scott, undertook the guardianship of the three boys, Turner, George and Edward. On the same day Major Thomas

Turner took Mary Jane off his hands, but not for long. Two months later Alexander Brown Scott and Mary Jane Dixon were married. This time there would be no misunderstanding. Scott demanded, and got, a marriage contract dated 27 December 1821. The property of Mary Jane Dixon would be enjoyed by her during her life, but, should she die, it would not revert to the Dixon estate.[8]

Mary Jane (Dixon) Scott promptly embarked on the course her mother had followed, childbirth in astonishingly rapid succession. Turner Dixon Scott was born in 1824, Robert in 1826, Marianna in 1828 and William in 1829. He was the last to be born alive. Her health broke under the strain.[9] The Dixon estate was still in a legal turmoil. In the years between 1821 and 1833 life at *Vermont* had become intolerable. The immense estate was one of the most fertile in Fauquier. There were platoons of Negroes, at least eighty (see Appendix E). As recalled by Edward Shacklett, one of the commissioners for the division of the land, the dower land alone was nearly 1,400 acres, and more than fifty Negroes were assigned to Mrs. Dixon. The change had apparently been gradual, but always for the worse. By 1833 a great many difficult problems had arisen, none of them easily solved.

In dividing the vast Dixon holdings in 1821, the Commissioners had been eminently fair. The eleven heirs each received 254 acres. Three got slightly more because their tracts included some undesirable land. The youngest, Alexander Dixon, was given 404 acres because his tract was detached from the rest and not easily subdivided. The dower lands awarded to the widow comprised 1,366 acres and included both the manor house *Vermont* and a mill.

The first of the Dixon male heirs, Henry Thomas Dixon, came of age in 1824. This may have been a source of relief to his guardian, Edward Brooke, Jr., because, to judge by later events, the young man must already have given some evidence of the violence and instability of character that marked his career. He may have removed himself from *Vermont* at this time, to the land he had received from his father's estate. There may be some significance in the fact that, within the limits of the Dixon estate, it was as far from the manor house as possible.

Turner Dixon, the next son, came of age in 1827. His ambition was to practice law, and he had no intention of remaining within the narrow confines of the Dixon Valley. He studied law at the University of Virginia and set up practice in Alexandria. Not much is known of him except that, 28 September 1831, he sold his inherited 254 acres to his younger brother,

Alexander Brown Scott
1790 - ca. 1852
Married daughters of Turner Dixon, Esq., Elizabeth Matilda Dixon and Mary Jane Dixon.

--courtesy of Mr. Taylor Chilton

George B. Dixon, for $6,500.[10] He figures only occasionally in the subsequent story of the Dixon family, when he employs his legal talents to foster friction among the heirs. He died in July 1864 and is buried in the Presbyterian Cemetery, Alexandria.

George Beverley Dixon came of age in 1828. On him fell the responsibility for the care of his own estate and those of his younger brothers. His task was further complicated by the now substantial evidence of their mother's growing insanity. There were periods of violence and acute manic depression. At times she was perfectly lucid, but those times were becoming increasingly rare. The evidence on record indicates that George B. Dixon was acquisitive, domineering and ruthless. At the same time one might well ask to what degree these unpleasant characteristics were forced upon him. Living on a farm with an insane mother, six younger brothers of whom three at least were to some degree unstable, and some eighty Negroes including several notable delinquents, was certainly no easy task.

In the first place, there was Edward Dixon, who was to reach his majority in 1831. He was already a chronic alcoholic, so much so that, on 31 March 1832, his brother was obliged to have the court declare him mentally incompetent in order to prevent his signing away his inheritance for money to buy liquor.[11] His brother-in-law, Richards Payne, states the case: "He was one of the most improvident, useless and extravagant men I have ever known." Even this harsh indictment is relatively mild beside the things that Edward Dixon said of his own conduct. In his long, rambling dissertation, Edward Dixon accuses his brother George of defrauding him of his birthright, his principal charge being that George did not save him from himself.[12]

The court later decided that George B. Dixon and his brother Henry did, in fact, purchase slaves from Edward's estate at ridiculously low prices. However, the temptation must have been great and can be justified somewhat on humanitarian grounds. It was said that the Negroes had always been together and that to sell them on the open market was not in the tradition of the society in which they lived.

The next problem to confront George B. Dixon was the estate of the next younger Dixon brother, William. This young man, who should have reached his majority in 1832, died under circumstances that are not revealed, before 2 November 1832. Then George Dixon sold most of William's share of his father's estate, more than 248 acres, to Miss Maria Willis. The mill and the remaining 34 acres he sold to James Morehead. Later, he was charged with never having distributed the proceeds of the sales among the heirs. The heirs had forgotten. He had, and was able to prove it.

On Major Thomas Turner of *Kinloch* had fallen the responsibility for his afflicted sister; her youngest daughter, Alice Fitzhugh Dixon; and guardianship of the four youngest Dixon boys, John, Charles C., Lucius, and Alexander. Trouble soon arose over what was alleged to be his refusal to hire out her slaves and his disastrous attempt to farm her dower lands. George B. Dixon appeared at *Kinloch* and summarily carted off his mother with her furniture and two old servants. The servants he unloaded on his sister, Mary Jane (Dixon) Scott at *Eastwood*. As the Dixon boys were still under age, another guardian was needed. John Dixon, nineteen in 1833, was apparently retarded. Obviously the new guardian had to be a man of substance, equipped to deal with a delicate and complicated situation. The guardian chosen was Peter Adams.

Adams soon observed that his young charges were almost completely without the benefit of education. He promptly arranged for Charles C. Dixon and Lucius Dixon, then fifteen and sixteen, to attend Tackett's School in Alexandria. A little later he sent the youngest, Alexander Dixon, to a school operated by Benjamin Hallowell in a remodeled sugar refinery on North Washington Street in the same city. About mid-term Lucius became tired of Tackett's (and, no doubt, they of him) and wanted to switch to Hallowell's. Peter Adams, who had paid his tuition for the entire year, said no.

In the meantime, on 1 May 1828, Henry Dixon sold his 254 acres to John Shumate.[13] We will learn much later of John Shumate, but this was the first of a series of purchases from the Dixon estate that would one day give Shumate possession of most of the upper one-third of the Dixon land. Henry presumably returned to live at *Vermont*--if he had ever left in the first place. *Vermont* was then "Bachelor Hall" and no tale that emanated from its precincts seemed improbable to the neighbors.

The year 1833 began for the Dixon family with fireworks on a rather grand scale. Early in January the night sky was illuminated by flames that consumed the house of a neighbor. It belonged to one Joshua Fletcher but was then occupied by Enos Withers Payne, his young wife and their infant daughter, Margaret. The Paynes escaped with their lives, but lost most of their possessions. It was charged that one of the Dixon Negroes with the improbable name of Tulip "did willfully and maliciously set fire to and burn down ... the said house," to the great discomfort of the occupants. Tulip said that she did not do it, but, in the Virginian concept of equal justice under the law prevailing at that period, her word had no value against that of a white person. She was found guilty.[14]

The penalty was hanging, but the court, suffering a twinge of conscience in the absence of any real evidence, recommended transportation to Africa instead. The state paid the Dixons three hundred dollars, her appraised value, out of which they paid Inman Horner, Esq. ten dollars for her defense.

The Dixons, however, had other things on their minds beside Tulip. Edward was bankrupt again. Turner wanted his money and Henry wanted control of the rich dower land of his mother. It was all too evident that she would never be able to decide anything concerning her estate. In fact, the doctor attending Mary Jane Scott during her pregnancies and increasing illness cautioned that it was dangerous to maintain a lunatic in a house with infant children. He urged that they make other arrangements. Reluctantly, they did so. The unhappy woman was sent to board with the family of Charles B. Stewart, then a tenant at *Vermont*.

This development stirred up a rather considerable amount of anxiety among the Dixon heirs, not so much concerning the fate of the poor woman as the fate of her 1,366 acres of valuable farmland and more than eighty Negroes. George B. Dixon had taken over as Committee for his mother on 21 February 1833, from Major Turner, but was unable to still the clamor for a liquidation of her assets. Henry T. Dixon and his brother, Turner Dixon, Jr., were undoubtedly the prime instigators of this rather unusual move, but they must have obtained the consent of the other heirs.

Therefore, on 21 February 1833, the representatives of Turner Dixon, deceased, presented a petition to the court for an act by the General Assembly of the Commonwealth of Virginia to allow them to divide her estate, including land and slaves "as if she were dead and intestate." Specifically it was provided that, should she recover her sanity, her estate would be returned to her. Furthermore, certain slaves were to be hired out, sufficient to maintain her, and the heirs were placed under bond to supplement that fund should the need arise. As might be expected, the need arose.[15]

The decree was handed down on 15 April 1833. Again, Alexander Brown Scott, in the right of his deceased first wife, Elizabeth Matilda Dixon, was ignored. Again he protested. This time he was successful and the court ordered the division in twelve equal parts instead of eleven as before stated.

Another and even more distressing complication had arisen. Mary Jane (Dixon) Scott, having had four children in rapid succession and with a fifth probably on the way, worn out by the care of her mother and anxiety over her family affairs, died at the age of twenty-eight. She made her will on the fourth of April and, within a month, was dead. Turner Dixon promptly contested the will on the grounds that it had not been witnessed. This time he lost. Frances T. Carter, Christian B. Scott, and Harriet Scott swore that they knew her handwriting and that it was unmistakably hers.[16]

She named her brother, George B. Dixon, as executor of her estate but he, for some reason, declined to serve. He then turned around and sued her estate for payment for nine acres, two roods and six poles of land which he claimed she had bought from him two years before.[17] Her substitute executor, Thomas T. Fauntleroy, had never heard of the sale. Her husband testified that she undoubtedly considered the land to be hers at the time of her death. The court awarded George B. Dixon $286 in payment for the land. When the survey accompanying the bill is plotted, it is found to be a thin sliver of land along the south boundary of the tract awarded Mary Jane (Dixon) Scott in the first division of her father's land. Furthermore, it lies wholly *within* the boundaries of that tract. One must suspect that George Dixon was taking advantage of the ignorance of the Scott heirs.

The commissioners appointed by the court to divide the dower land of Maria Dixon were Thomas Marshall of *Oak Hill*, son of the Chief Justice; his brother, James Keith Marshall; and John Shumate. Sensibly, they employed the man who had made the original survey under the supervision of the elder Charles Kemper to make the division. He was Charles Duncan and he must have had a difficult time of it. Not only was the dower property of irregular shape, but each heir must have both cleared land and woodland. The result was a number of small properties, some adjacent to the individual heir's original allotment and others far removed. Many years were to pass before they could be reassembled into several more or less contiguous estates. Surprisingly, he accomplished his task according to the first decree in a little more than two months. Seven weeks later the second decree was handed down altering the division of the property from eleven to twelve equal shares. It is not clear how that was managed, but the adjustment was probably made in securities and slaves, rather than by re-doing Duncan's complicated division of land.

As the division of the dower land was intended to permit the heirs to pursue their separate courses, it is interesting to see what each of them did with their added inheritance. Even before the estate was settled on 10 November 1834, a large part of it had changed hands. This, as nearly as can be determined from court records, is what happened: The individual heirs each received upwards of 105 acres in addition to the 254 or more already given them. Had all things been equal, each would have had a fine farm of more than 360 acres, a dozen or so slaves and adequate capital to operate it. However:

    Henry Thomas Dixon, having sold his share of the original tract division to John Shumate in 1828, had only his share of the dower tract. He wanted the manor house, *Vermont*, and before November of 1833 he had persuaded his brothers, George B. and the feckless Edward, to throw in their dower rights with his. In the final settlement he awarded the house and 314 1/2 acres. He was married in Washington County, Maryland, to Annie E. Brown of Berkeley County, Virginia, (now W. Va.) on 1 January 1835. On 6 September 1836, Henry T. Dixon and Annie, his wife, sold *Vermont* and 314 1/2 acres to James Rogers.[18] In the deal was included 51 1/2 acres he had bought in from his brother Charles and 101 acres outside the Dixon estate bought from John Marshall, Jr. Thus, only two years after the settlement of the estate, *Vermont* passed out of the hands of the Dixons forever. With the house gone, the rest was soon to follow.

    Mary Jane (Dixon) Scott died, of course, during the settlement. She died at *Eastwood* on the 254-acre tract she had obtained from the first division. Obviously her estate gained nothing from the 9 acres allegedly purchased from George B. Dixon in November of 1831. In the division of the dower land the children of Alexander Brown Scott were given 105 acres. This makes a total of 359 acres. However, when her estate was divided among her four children as described in a chancery suit between 1849 and 1859, there were 394 acres.[19] The 35-acre surplus was purchased at an unknown date from a tract of land east of the Orlean-Salem Road.

    Turner Dixon, the Alexandria lawyer, sold the 254 acres he received in the original division to his brother George in 1831. Upon receipt of an additional 123 acres from the dower division, he sold that with equal promptness on 15 April 1834 to James Morehead whose property it adjoined. Turner Dixon was also married at this time. His wife was Mary Jane Paton, daughter of John B. Paton of Alexandria. He died in July 1864 and is buried with his wife in the Presbyterian Cemetery. Their only child to reach maturity, William P. Dixon, died while a student at William and Mary College, 31 May 1857.

    George Beverley Dixon had 254 acres from the original division. To that he added another 254 acres in 1831 by purchase from his brother Turner. However he sold a little more than 24 acres of his new purchase to John Shumate on 27 March 1832. He received one-tenth of the dower land of his mother, about 105 acres, but this he sold or gave to his brother Henry T. Dixon. At that time he should have had left about 484 acres.

In the spring of 1835, he decided to try his fortunes elsewhere. On 26 October 1835, he conveyed 225 acres of his home place, *Westwood*, to Thomas L. Maddux.[20] On the same day, he conveyed 163 acres of his purchase from Turner Dixon to Samuel Bayley.[21] The remaining 96 acres he apparently sold to John Shumate, though record of that sale has not been found. Before 9 June 1836, he was in Adams County, Mississippi.

George B. Dixon had an interest in a store in Salem (now Marshall) which he operated in partnership with William Shields. Both Shields and Dixon sold their interests to Daniel R. Flowerree in 1836. In the deed to Flowerree, Dixon's wife's name appears as "Conisande." However, Adams County records show that he married Cariasande Grady (or Crercy).[22] On 12 October 1837, he signed a release in a lawsuit brought by his brother Edward. In a deposition he stated that he was married in June of 1836. In a letter addressed to his brother, Henry T. Dixon, he said that he had moved from Natchez to Yazoo City in central Mississippi and had lost his entire fortune. In connection with that loss he speaks of a James P. Creecy, a name somewhat like that of his supposed wife. Henry Dixon, in a burst of unwonted generosity, suggested that he return to Virginia and stay with him. Knowing his brother's mercurial temperament, George declined. In November of 1842, George B. Dixon was declared bankrupt in Yazoo County, Mississippi. It is doubtful that he remained to receive this final humiliation.

It is therefore rather startling to read in the *National Intelligencer* (Washington, D.C.) that George B. Dixon of Mississippi, and Mary B. McDonald of Edenton, North Carolina, were married at Edenton, 13 March 1844. Even more surprising is the news, also from the *National Intelligencer*, that Alexander Dixon of Warrenton, Virginia, and Corissande E. McDonald, daughter of General Duncan McDonald of Edenton, North Carolina, were married at Edenton, 4 July 1844. The same minister officiated at both ceremonies. The story behind this sequence of events remains obscure.

As George B. Dixon was a "Committee of the Person and Estate of Maria Dixon, a Lunatic," at the time of his planned departure for Mississippi, he rendered an accounting before he left Fauquier, dated 9 April 1835. She had remained with the Scotts at *Eastwood* only seven months. Henry Dixon, as soon as he acquired *Vermont*, took her there, and she remained in his household until her death. On 28 September 1835, Henry Dixon was appointed "Committee, etc.," over the protest of the rest of the family, who wanted Richards Payne, an attorney recently married to their sister Alice instead.

Edward Dixon "regained the use of his faculties" long enough in 1833 to have his share of the original division of the Dixon estate, 254 acres, restored to him. On 31 October 1833, he sold it to Andrew Barbee for $4,000. He later complained that his brother George had "suffered" him to make an "incautious" sale. In fact, he was deeply in debt and there was no other alternative. He promptly lapsed into what he, himself, described as his "extravagant and ruinous course ... urged on by the excitement of constant intemperance." His condition was well enough known so that he could obtain no credit in the neighborhood except from the store in which his brother George was a partner.

When the division of the dower lands was made, Edward was apparently in some hazy world of his own. Later he accused George of having appropriated the 104 acres that represented his share. The record shows that George's "arts and wiles" were certainly not turned to his own "exclusive advantage." In fact, on the same day that he sold his property to Barbee, he had deeded one-tenth of the dower estate of his mother to his brother Henry T. Dixon. On 7 December 1836, Edward Dixon filed suit against George B. Dixon alleging that during the period of one year he was "left destitute in the world without means of obtaining the poorest subsistence." It was decided that George should pay him $350, as the difference between the value of some slaves he had bought of Edward and the amount the latter had demanded.

Having obtained as much as he could from George, Edward next sued his brother Henry. While "in great distress for money with which to purchase the necessities of life" he had sold slaves to Henry for $400 though they were worth more. At the time he was so "disrupted" that he did not realize that he was being cheated. The court annulled the sale, provided that Edward or someone for him could come up with $400 with interest from 1840 (it was then 1846), within ninety days. If the slaves were indeed worth more, as alleged, it is probable that someone did raise the money and Edward did realize a small profit on their sale. The record does not say. After that day, 10 October 1846, Edward Dixon simply drifted off the pages of recorded history, a penniless, worthless drunk. His brother-in-law, Richards Payne, provided what subsistence he had during the rest of his life.[23]

Alice Fitzhugh (Dixon) Payne
1812 - 1900
Daughter of Turner and Maria (Turner) Dixon and wife of Richards Payne, Esq.

--courtesy of Mrs. Elizabeth W. Lindley

William Dixon, of course, died before the second division. He received 280 acres in the first division which were sold by his brother George as commissioner for the sale of his estate. Two hundred forty-eight acres went to Miss Maria Willis, 2 November 1832, and the remaining land with the mill to James Morehead the same day.[24] The proceeds were distributed between his brothers and sister. As the same distribution would apply to anything received from the dower division, his estate was not included in that transaction.

Alice Fitzhugh (Dixon) Payne was unmarried in 1833. She had received 254 acres from the original division and was given 78 acres of cleared land and 60 acres of woodland in the dower division, making a total of 392 acres. On 17 September 1834, she married Richards Payne in Warrenton. It was, according to the Payne Bible, "a cloudy day, a happy couple." Richards Payne, in addition to being happy, was also brave, considering what he must have known of his bride's family. He was the second son of Daniel and Elizabeth Hooe (Winter) Payne of *Granville* near Warrenton. He was a lawyer by profession, which certainly was a great advantage in his subsequent dealings with the Dixon family. Most of his efforts on their behalf earned him nothing but their enmity.[25]

Perhaps to minimize their involvement in troublesome family matters, they sold all of Mrs. Payne's share of her father's estate on 11 August 1838 to James Morehead.[26] At that time she had 418 1/4 acres. How she came by the additional 26 acres is unrecorded. A certain amount of shifting about of property boundaries apparently occurred within the family without recorded deeds.

John Dixon was nineteen in 1833. He received 315 acres from the first division. In the dower division he received 100 acres of cleared land and 23 1/2 acres of woodland, making a total 438 1/2 acres. On 28 January 1833, the court appointed Peter Adams as his guardian. When he came of age in 1835, the court, taking cognizance of the fact that he was mentally incompetent, continued the guardianship. His entire estate was placed in trust with Peter Adams, 8 September 1835, to provide for his modest needs and to board him with a congenial family, "not in a town or publick tavern or such like places," for the remainder of his life.[27] He died in 1843.[28]

On 31 August 1849, Richards Payne, as administrator of John's estate distributed the proceeds of its sale to his brothers and sister, except Lucius, who could not be found.[29] John Dixon's share of the Dixon property became *Silver Spring* a fine farm in the Dixon Valley.[30]

Charles C. Dixon, aged eighteen in 1833, was one of the three youngest Dixon sons for whom Peter Adams was appointed guardian in a single court order dated 28 January 1833. He received 254 acres of the original division and three small tracts in the dower division, 51 1/2 acres of cleared land, 66 acres of woodland and 17 acres in a narrow triangle that appears to have been left over from an earlier sale to James Morehead. After he came of age in 1836 it took him less than two months to find a purchaser for most of his land. On 22 August 1836, he sold to George Adams three parcels totaling 337 acres.[31] This and adjacent purchases outside the original Dixon estate became *Moreland*. Charles C. Dixon was already in Mississippi, probably with his brother George, when this sale was made. He sold the 51 1/2 acres of cleared land, which was not contiguous, to his brother Henry who promptly resold it to James Rogers.

In the spring of 1835 Alexander Dixon, writing from Alexandria to the wife of his brother Henry, was concerned as to Charles's whereabouts. George B. Dixon, upon hearing that Charles had refused to go to the university, had asked him to go to "south" with him, but apparently had to leave without him. Charles seems, though, to have joined his brother later. He settled in Benton, Mississippi, a hamlet some ten miles east of Yazoo. There, according to a report in the *National Intelligencer*, we learn that "Charles C. Dixon, son of the late Turner Dixon of Fauquier County, died at Benton, Mississippi, 17 May 1841, in the 26th year of his age."

It is, therefore, surprising to read a letter dated September 1842 from Benton, Mississippi, from Charles C. Dixon to his brother Henry. He writes unequivocally, "I have lost all I had, and owe more than I ever expect to be able to pay." (We also have a 1978 letter from a lady living in Mississippi who gives convincing evidence that he married and died there about 1872 at the age of fifty-seven, leaving one daughter. The lady says that his name was Charles Christian Dixon and that she is his granddaughter.)

Lucius Dixon, aged seventeen in 1833, received 265 acres in the initial division. To this was added in 1833, three parcels, 126 acres of cleared land, a small wooded lot containing 30 acres and another wooded lot containing 60 acres; a total of 480 acres. Peter Adams was his guardian until he came of age on the tenth of September 1837. On 27 November 1843, Lucius Dixon sold all of his inherited land. To John Shumate went 223 1/2 acres of his original lot, 19 1/2 acres of the 60-acre woodland tract and 2 acres of the smaller tract; a total of 245 acres.[32] To his nephew, Turner Dixon Scott, then only nineteen years old, he sold the remainder of his original lot and the cleared land from the dower division. To this was added 40 acres of the larger wooded lot and 28 acres of the smaller, making a total of 235 acres. Shumate was to pay $4,900 and Scott $4,700, but not immediately. In fact, six years later, exclusive of interest, Shumate had paid only $400 and Scott virtually nothing.[33]

> **LAND FOR SALE.**
>
> The Subscriber will sell his farm in the County of Fauquier, lying at the Eastern base of the Cobler Mountain. It was a portion of the Vermont estate which fell to the subscriber in the division of the land of the late Turner Dixon among his children. It lies adjoining the tract recently purchased by James Rogers of Loudoun County.
>
> The tract contains
>
> 480 ACRES,
>
> more than a hundred acres of which is heavily timbered. The open land is in good tilth and farming condition. The improvements consist of a good overseers house and comfortable negro cabins.— The whole farm is well watered and well adapted to grazing.
>
> There is a spring of Chalybeate water of great strength, near the place which should be selected for the dwelling house, which adds great value to the land. Its medicinal effects are known and for years have been highly appreciated throughout that whole region of country.
>
> Persons wishing to purchase, are refered to Peter Adams Esquire Oak Hill, who is authorized to sell, and will shew the premises.
>
> LUCIUS DIXON.
>
> December 2, 1837—3mo.
>
> Leesburg Washingtonian will publish the above three months.

The "chalybeate" spring still flows in Dixon's Valley.

There is no question that, of the Dixon children, Lucius Dixon, was the most erratic, unpredictable and self-destructive. He seemed to have every advantage: good-looks, charm of manner, wealth, education and social position. In fact, he was moody, introverted, passionate and irresponsible. Certainly he was not without intelligence. He attended the University of Virginia and was, in the summer of 1847, on his way to Philadelphia to qualify for entrance in a medical school, probably the University of Pennsylvania, then generally considered the finest in the nation.

On 22 September 1847, he married Rosina Ashton, the 18-year-old daughter of Henry Washington Ashton of *Ashley*, near Warrenton. Her father was of an old and distinguished family and was, in fact, a cousin of Alexander B. Scott. Her mother was Anne Allason Rose, daughter of Captain Robert and Mary Seymour (Hooe) Rose.[34] Their eldest son, Arthur Ashton, had been a longtime friend of Lucius Dixon. Lucius Dixon had courted Rosina assiduously, though he claimed that it was the other way around, and that he had been forced into marriage by the machinations of her parents and the Scotts. He blamed especially Marianna Scott, his niece. Marianna was simply engaging in that perennial avocation dear to every female heart--matchmaking. Poor girl! She had not planned on reaping the whirlwind.

From the wild, passionate, and often incoherent letters introduced into court, it appears evident that he had no business being married at all, certainly not to Rosina Ashton. After a humiliating month at *Ashley* she went with him to Philadelphia, where after two weeks of neglect and brutality, she had enough. He visited Warrenton several times during the winter, sometimes without letting her know, at other times insisting on meeting her at the home of her grandmother. His bitterness toward her mother appears almost psychotic. Writing from Philadelphia, he knows that entrance to medical school will be denied him and proposes living in Caroline County below Fredericksburg near his "dearest" relatives. They were two bachelor uncles, presumably brothers of his mother, as his father had no brothers. Next, he was going to lose himself in the western wilderness, living in a cabin with a dirt floor, with his only friend, Aunt Ruth, a faithful Negro slave. He thought of suicide, anything to "break the heart of that damned old bitch ... [for which] I would agree to suffer in Hell a thousand years."[35]

He carried out none of his threats, but, of course, when he appeared in Fauquier County in March refusing to promise to keep the peace with Ashton and his family, he was clapped into jail.[36] Richards Payne had him released on bond, after which he disappeared. In December Arthur Ashton testified that he was last heard of in Missouri in April, and was reported on his way to Mexico. Why Mexico? The treaty ending the war with Mexico had been signed in February 1848, and the name was on everyone's tongue. It was another of his threats.

Rosina (Ashton) Dixon received her decree of divorce in the June court, 1849, with alimony and the custody of the child, Anne Ashton Dixon, called Nannie. In December 1855, the will of Lucius was submitted to the court for probate. Because it was promptly contested by the attorneys for his wife, probate was denied. We are therefore unable to determine how or where he died. He was only thirty-eight.

Alexander Dixon, sixteen in 1833, was the youngest of the Dixon heirs. In the first division of the Dixon estate he received by far the largest dividend, 404 acres, across the road that formed the eastern boundary of the other Dixon property. To this was added a little more than 111 acres in the dower division. When he came of age on 30 November 1838, he took possession of a fine property totaling 515 acres of splendid farmland. The following year he sold all of it.

On 29 May 1839, he sold to Marshall Jett 315 1/2 acres on the east side of the Salem-Orlean Road which he described as "corner to Lucius and Alexander Dixon's 100-acre lot."[37] The part sold to Jett was composed of the Daniel F. Payne lease which his father had purchased from John Marshall in 1814 and the land he bought from William Rust in 1817. It would appear that these tracts supposed to contain 304 acres were, when resurveyed, nearer 315 acres. Also mentioned in his deed to Jett was "his interest in the land west of the Salem-Orlean road." Apparently the land to the west, received as part of his allotment from the first division he had, by some private agreement, offered to share with his brother Lucius. *Mount Jett* was built by Marshall Jett on the tract east of the road.

On 22 July he sold the land he received from the dower division, computed as 112 1/2 acres, to James Rogers, who had bought *Vermont* which it adjoined.[38] On 29 November, having presumably obtained a release from his brother, he sold the "100 acre lot" to John Shumate.[39] As it turned out it measured only 98 3/4 acres. For all his land Alexander Dixon netted only $7,350, low even for that time.

After Peter Adams sent him to Hallowell's School in Alexandria, Alexander attended the University of Virginia in the autumn of 1836/37 with the hope of studying medicine. That hope lasted for one semester. He intended to go "south" and join his brother George B. Dixon, but the latter's financial ruin in Yazoo County, Mississippi, ended those plans. On 26 January 1844, when he was twenty-seven, he unburdened the story of his unhappy life in the chancery suit brought by the Dixon heirs against Henry T. Dixon for an accounting of their mother's estate. One hopes that the *National Intelligencer* is correct in stating that he married Corissande E. McDonald on the fourth of July of that year in Edenton, North Carolina, and that he lived happily ever after. We do not know.

* * *

So ends the turbulent history of *Vermont* in the days of the Dixons. Our further history concerns itself with the colorful history of the people who took over these same lands after the Dixons had departed. But no story of the Dixon family would be complete without some further mention of Henry Thomas Dixon who was to gain eternal fame as "the only man in Fauquier County to vote for Abraham Lincoln."[40]

After the sale of *Vermont* in 1836, he bought a fine farm called *Milan* near Rectortown. There he moved his family, including his invalid mother, for whose estate he was now fully responsible. He also owned, for a time, an estate known as *Tip Top* (now *Courtney*) near Delaplane. However, he was living with his family in Upperville when, in November of 1847, death finally released his unfortunate mother from a lifetime of misery.[41]

The protracted litigation over the remains of his mother's estate only estranged him still further from his family, and his harsh and arrogant conduct lost him most of those who might have been his friends. For a while before 28 July 1856, he was actually confined in the Western Asylum for the Insane at Staunton, Virginia. Part of his estate was placed in the hands of William H. Hume, the county sheriff. On the above date the court certified that he was cured, but within a month had cause to regret that action.[42]

In default of braver men, Dr. Thomas Clay Maddux, who had grown up at *Westwood* (land bought by his father from Dixon's brother, George B. Dixon), volunteered to arrest Dixon's eldest son on charges of brutally assaulting a young man at an Upperville bar.[43] Henry Dixon shot him in the shoulder, inflicting a painful wound from which he never fully recovered. Dixon later boasted that he would one day finish the job.

On 6 November 1860, Henry Thomas Dixon presented himself at the polling place in Salem, Fauquier County* and loudly proclaimed his support for Abraham Lincoln. Today it might be argued that he did so from the highest moral principles--a profound hatred for slavery and a true reverence for the Union. That possibility did not occur to anyone at the time. Henry Dixon was just being his old ornery self and, though surprised, people reasoned that it "figured." Regardless, Dixon achieved the sensation he doubtless desired.[44]

He did not endear himself further, as far as his neighbors were concerned, when he promptly joined the Union army.

---

* Another source says "Markham Precinct."

Thomas Clay Maddux, M.D.
Son of Thomas L. and Dorcas (Davis) Maddux of *Westwood*

--courtesy of George R. Thompson III

He was a man of commanding presence, articulate, and—when he wanted to be—engaging. He was given a commission as major and soon reached the office of regimental paymaster. He did not, however, win the confidence of his superiors, and his wife's comings and goings through enemy lines with apparent ease excited suspicion on both sides.

After hostilities had ceased Major Dixon was stationed in Alexandria. Dr. Maddux was also in town. It was rumored about Alexandria that Major Dixon was gunning for him. Maddux decided that this had gone on long enough. The showdown came on 10 November 1865, outside the City Hotel, adjoining Gadsby's Tavern in Alexandria.[45] There was some question as to who fired the first shot, but no question as to which was the better marksman. Major Dixon died the following morning, loudly insisting that Maddux had shot him before he had drawn his pistol. He was the only witness who maintained that point of view. Maddux had no trouble convincing the jury that, had he not fired first, he himself would have been the victim.*

Major Dixon was buried in Alexandria with suitable honors. In July 1895, his remains were removed to Arlington Cemetery where he sleeps today under a much-worn, hardly legible headstone.[46] Mrs. Dixon died on 13 February 1899. Her funeral was conducted in the midst of a blinding blizzard. One wonders how they got her coffin across the Potomac Bridge. Faithful through thick and thin, she rests beside her husband. Her gravestone, in contrast to that of her husband, is of polished granite and looks new.[47]

Lewis Edmonds Payne, who knew Dixon well, wrote of him in 1879 with the grudging admiration everyone holds for the perfect villain.[48] "Like Atilla the Hun," he wrote, "he came into the world to disturb it. He was not a bad-looking man, of powerful physique, with small, dark eyes twinkling with malicious humor. His heart bore malice as the flint does the fire. He had a peculiar twang that gave his voice infernal meanness. A knife run through him would have had a chill. He possessed a rare intellect, a various versatile, vigorous mind and prostituted it to the vilest uses. His tongue was a flaming rapier ... and peeled the skin from the sensitive as lightning barks a tree. He had little fear of man, the law or the devil; and lived at thrust point with the world." He was, in fact, Payne wrote, "an original, *sui generis*."

---

* For an account of Dr. Maddux's untimely fate, see Appendix C.

Notes for Chapter 2

1. W. P. A. of Virginia, Historical Inventory, Research by Frances B. Foster, 6 May 1937, *Vermont*.
2. Fauquier County Deed Book 20, p. 244,
3. *ibid*.
4. *ibid*., Deed Book 21, p. 275.
5. Turner Dixon served as the second Postmaster at Salem (now Marshall) for one year, 1819-1820. On 28 June 1813 Turner Dixon, Esq'r. "came into Court and in open Court took the several oaths required by law to be taken by Justices of peace and took his seat upon the Bench."
6. Fauquier County Will Book 12, p. 212.
7. Fauquier County Guardian Bonds, 1818-1871.
8. Fauquier County Deed Book 26, p. 140.
9. Fauquier County Will Book 13, p. 64.
10. Fauquier County Deed Book 32, p. 339. Turner Dixon was a classmate of Edgar Allan Poe at the Unversity of Virginia during the session February to December 1826. Poe left an account of Dixon's "feudistic affair" with a fellow student, which nearly ended in tragedy for young Dixon. He was saved when his opponent's pistol misfired. See: Hervey Allen, "Israfel." (N.Y., Doran, 1927), p. 160.
11. Fauquier County Order Book 1832-34, p. 45.
12. Chancery Suit #46, styled "E. Dixon vs. G. B. Dixon."
13. Fauquier County Deed Book 31, p. 34.
14. Fauquier County Order Book 1832-34, pp. 207, 224.
15. Chancery Suit, Ex Parte Dixon #10.
16. Fauquier County Will Book 13, p. 64.
17. Chancery Suit #5, styled "Dixon vs. Scott."
18. Fauquier County Deed Book 38, p. 364, "excepting the graveyard on the *Vermont* tract which the said Henry T. Dixon hereby reserves to himself and his heirs forever."
19. Chancery Suit #133, styled "Scott vs. Scott."
20. Fauquier County Deed Book 35, p. 325.

21. *ibid.*, p. 326.
22. Letter from Norman E. Gillis, Shreveport, La., to John K. Gott, 30 January 1978. The Yazoo Banner, Benton, Mississippi, dated 14 July 1838, carried the following obituary: Died at her residence in this co. on Sunday, the 1st, Mrs. Carissande Dixon, consort of George B. Dixon, Esq. and only daughter of James R. Creecy, Esq., of Manchester."
23. Chancery Suit #61, styled "E. Dixon vs. H. T. Dixon." Another source says that Edward Dixon was an editor with the U. S. Charge d'Affaires, in Bogota, Columbia, South America and that he died in 1854 in Caroline County, Va.
24. Fauquier County Deed Book 33, p. 336; D. B. 34, p. 79.
25. Brooke Payne, *The Paynes of Virqinia*, (Richmond, 1937), p. 138.
26. Fauquier County Deed Book 38, p. 277.
27. Fauquier County Deed Book 35, p. 314.
28. Fauquier County Order Book 1843-46, p. 132.
29. Fauquier County Will Book 22, p. 289.
30. Fauquier County Deed Book 44, p. 221.
31. Fauquier County Deed Book 36, p. 302.
32. Fauquier County Deed Book 43, p. 399.
33. Chancery Suit #155, styled "R. Dixon vs. L. Dixon"
34. Hayden, *Virginia Genealoqies*, p. 631.
35. Letter from Lucius Dixon to Rosina Dixon, filed in Chancery Suit #155, *op. cit.*
36. Fauquier County Minute Book 1846-49, p. 236.
37. Fauquier County Deed Book 39, p. 119.
38. *ibid.*, p. 154.
39. *ibid.*, p. 284.
40. B. Curtis Chappelear, *Maps and Notes Pertaining to the Upper Section of Fauquier County, Virginia*, (Warrenton: The Warrenton Antiquarian Society, 1954), p. 11. Southern claims file, National Archives, Annie E. Dixon, no. 21238
41. Chancery Suit #76, styled "M. Dixon vs. H. T. Dixon" (1844-1856), Fredericksburg District Court.
42. Fauquier County Minute Book 1856-57, p. 114.
43. Fauquier County Minute Book 1856-57, pp. 170, 236, 266. "Commonwealth vs. Collins Dixon."
44. Chancery Suit #228, styled "Scott vs. Dixon." Major Richard H. Carter testified in 1871 in this suit that Major Dixon, whom he knew very well, told him in April 1861, in Washington, D. C., that he (Dixon) never expected to return to Virginia and "it would give him pleasure to fire the first cannon towards Virginia."
45. *The Alexandria Gazette* (Alexandria, Va.), 28 October 17 - November 1865.

46. Arlington National Cemetery, Records, Section 1, Lot 683. The Dixons are buried near the gate at the Fort Myer Chapel entrance to the cemetery.
47. *The Evening Star* (Washington, D. C.), 4 February 1899.
48. *Alexandria Gazette* (Alexandria, Va.) 25 August 1879. From "A Letter from Fauquier." Lewis Edmonds Payne was a son of Dr. Alban Smith Payne of *Granville* near Markham. He attended Edwards Academy with Dixon's son, Henry Thomas Dixon, Jr.

3

Vermont
1839 - 1978

There was room in the vast and beautiful Dixon Valley for many splendid farms. From the immense Dixon tract were carved the following:

Vermont, later *Glenara*
Eastwood
Westwood
White House
Silver Spring
Bleak House
The Shumate Place
Mount Jett
Cleveland, later *Piedmont Farm*
Vernon Mills
much of Moreland

and others of lesser size. The history of these places and the people who lived in them is interesting, but even more so is the history of the land and what happened to it. The oldest inhabited site on the Dixon tract is, of course, *Glenara* where *Vermont* once stood.

Not much is known of James Rogers and Martha, his wife, who bought *Vermont* from Henry T. Dixon in 1836. They lived quietly, kept their fences in repair, paid their taxes and did not permit their servants to burn down their neighbors' houses. They came from Loudoun County where a Rogers family was prosperous and equally reticent about their antecedents.[1] In addition to the 314.5 acre *Vermont* estate, they bought Charles C. Dixon's 51.5 acre tract adjoining, in 1836. On 22 July 1839, they added Alexander Dixon's 112.5 acre dower division. Then, in 1844, they bought a corner of *Mount Jett* from Marshall Jett.[2] It was known as Bastables Corner and contained 79 acres, 1 rood, 13 7/10 poles.

Possibly with a bit of arm-twisting they were persuaded to buy 100.5 acres which Henry Dixon happened to own in the Free State. As the Free State is a mythical land, its exact location is unknown. It was too small to farm easily, so they added to it 145 acres from James Edward Marshall.

Then, almost twenty years after their arrival, James and Martha Rogers departed as quietly as they had come. On 13 October 1855, they deeded all of their property to Benjamin F. Rixey. *Vermont* then contained 471 acres, 7.5 acres having disappeared somehow. Rixey bought Bastables Corner and the Free State land as well. James Rogers and Martha, his wife, later lived in Loudoun and Culpeper Counties; he died in the latter place in 1883.[3]

The new owner of *Vermont* was as flamboyant as the Rogers had been quiet and unassuming. Benjamin F. Rixey's family had long been established in Culpeper County, where the village of Rixeyville preserves the name. His grandfather had married Elizabeth Morehead, daughter of the first John Morehead of Fauquier who died in 1768. Thereafter, the Rixeys had been associated by blood and marriage with the Morehead family whose land tenure within the Dixon Valley was as long as that of the Dixons themselves.[4]

His grandfather, called Richard Rixey Jr., bought *Grafton*, the property directly north of the Turner Dixon tract, 11 January 1800. It had originally been part of the Mercer tract which Colonel Thomas Harrison had bought and left to his son Burr. Burr Harrison sold it in 1775 and it had changed hands several times before it came to Catesby Graham, who sold it to Rixey. It contained 204.75 acres. On 24 September 1804, Richard Rixey deeded it to his son, Captain Samuel Rixey (1780-1866) who built the present house. On 6 June 1809, Captain Rixey married Frances Downing Morehead, born 1779, daughter of Presley and Elizabeth (Hunton) Morehead. As Presley Morehead was a son of his grandmother's brother, Charles Morehead, he and his wife were cousins.

Captain Samuel Rixey and his wife lived at *Grafton* until 1817. Five of his children were born there, but not Benjamin F. Rixey, who was the youngest. He and his brother, John William Hunton Rixey, were born at *Hilly Farm* in Culpeper County. Benjamin F. Rixey was born on 3 October 1821. The family never lost its love for the Dixon Valley, though, or the desire to own some of its fertile acres, the best place for horse-breeding, said Benjamin Rixey, in the world. It therefore came as no surprise when, on 7 January 1845, he married Eleanora Morehead. Eleanora Morehead was the only daughter of Captain James Morehead and his first wife, Ann Johnson.

Benjamin Franklin Rixey
1821-1884

Through purchases and the dower of his wife, Eleanora (Morehead) Rixey, Mr. Rixey was able to re-assemble most of the Dixons' *Vermont*. Following the Civil War, this fine estate could not produce enough to repay the vast debts against it. Much of the estate was thus sold, including the site of the *Vermont* house. When the purchaser decided not to keep the original house, Mr. Rixey contracted to have the building removed about a mile north to a lovely grove of oaks. The tale is told that he fortified himself with a barrel of whiskey, ensconced himself in the parlor and made the trip across the fields to the new site, arriving in one month.

Vermont, the Home of Benjamin Franklin Rixey

At the time of his marriage Benjamin F. Rixey was apparently living at *Bleak House*, on a 166-acre tract, part of a larger tract in the Turner Dixon grant sold by Lucius Dixon to John Shumate two years before. He also had a half interest in a tract of 615.5 acres purchased from Gilbert M. Bastable and split between his cousin, Smith H. Rixey, and himself. It lay directly across the Salem-Orlean Road from *Bleak House*. (See BLEAK HOUSE.)

When Captain James Morehead died in January of 1847 he left a large landed estate of which Eleanora Rixey inherited 156 acres. In addition, Benjamin F. Rixey bought the land inherited by his wife's brothers, James Milton and Armistead H. Morehead, in March of 1852.[5] The first purchase was really a swap, as he deeded *Bleak House* to James Milton Morehead, 16 March 1852.[6] By that time he had 505 acres of the Morehead property. Presumably the Rixeys then moved to *Mountain View*. Three years later he bought *Vermont*, increasing his holdings within the original Dixon grant to 976 acres.

That was apparently not enough. At an unknown date Benjamin Rixey bought the rest of the Morehead land from DeWit Clinton Morehead, 201 acres. On 7 January 1850, he bought three tracts from Turner Dixon Scott, son of Alexander B. and Mary Jane (Dixon) Scott.[7] The first of these, 166+ acres was land Scott had bought from Lucius Dixon in 1843. It adjoined land of John Shumate and *Vermont*, then owned by the Rogers. The second tract of 40 acres was part of Lucius Dixon's old wood lot from the dower division of 1833. The third tract was 28 acres out of the 30 acres of woodland also allotted to Lucius Dixon in 1833. This last tract Rixey immediately resold to Nathaniel G. Carter as it did not adjoin his other land.[8] The net gain to the Rixey estate was, therefore, 206 acres.

Taking all into account--*Vermont* (472 acres), the land Rogers had bought from Marshall Jett (79.5 acres), the land in the Free State Rogers had bought from Henry Dixon (245.5 acres), the Morehead land (716 acres)--Benjamin F. Rixey owned 1,513 acres of land in 1861, plus several smaller pieces of which the exact date of purchase is unknown. During the decade before the war, the Rixeys lived in considerable style. The acquisition of land was in Benjamin Rixey's blood and, as he saw his other assets wilt in the conflict that followed, he reasoned, not without sense, that the land would always be there, come what may.

As we have seen, John Shumate had, over a period of years, been buying parts of the Dixon estate and owned a considerable acreage, mostly at the north end of the old Turner

Dixon grant. He had also bought a 223-acre tract from Lucius Dixon lying along the east side of the Dixon grant, along the road from Marshall to Orlean, and several other minor pieces. This farm totaled 315.25 acres when Benjamin Rixey bought it on 30 December 1863 from John Shumate and John T. Jones, presumably for Confederate currency and a mortgage. Subsequently, at an unknown date, he bought another 190 acres from John Shumate. He now owned more than 2,000 acres. When the war was over he had a total of 2,199 acres counting 71 additional acres he had picked up in the Free State and a little more than 100 acres in miscellaneous small tracts.

Through the long, relentless war the Rixeys lived at *Vermont* between hope and fear that ultimately became despair. Though they had no sons of fighting age, their families on both sides were irrevocably committed to the Confederate cause. William Morehead was killed at Yellow Tavern. Richard H. Rixey, with Mosby's Rangers, lived dangerously. Milton Morehead, 2nd lieutenant in Wise's Dragoons, was in constant peril. They watched in helpless anger as their magnificent farmland was laid waste, their fences destroyed, their cattle and livestock plundered. They lost a fortune in Negroes, most of whom departed, leaving behind the old and sick. These the Rixeys could not bear to turn away, though they had not enough food to feed themselves. A poignant glimpse of the scene around them is found in "Years of Anguish," a collection of letters and diaries of their friends and neighbors of Fauquier County.

Yet, from all this Benjamin F. Rixey emerged with a curious optimism. It was true that there was no money left, the slaves were gone and the buildings were half in ruins, but the land was there, as fertile as ever. With a few years of diligent effort, his fortunes, he believed, could be restored. He was to the manor born and had never known want before the war. Soon the wounds would be healed and the Rixeys would come to their own again.

Believing it the duty of men of his class to take part in politics and lend a voice of experience in the rehabilitation of his ravaged state, Rixey ran for the Virginia House of Delegates in 1865 and served two years. Again, in 1871, he represented Fauquier and Rappahannock Counties in the state senate, "having been elected to fill the vacancy caused by the resignation of Thomas N. Latham." He was, of course, an ardent Democrat, a view which led him into a violent altercation with Colonel John Singleton Mosby, the intrepid Partisan leader.

After the war Mosby's convoluted mind had followed a rather peculiar bent. He had become a warm admirer of General Ulysses S. Grant and a supporter of his candidacy for reelection to the presidency in 1872. This left most of his Fauquier County adherents dumbfounded. Two years later, in the congressional election of 1874, Mosby announced that he would run as an independent against the highly esteemed General Eppa Hunton. He was thus actively seeking votes to go to Congress to support a man who, seven years earlier, had vowed to "hang him by the neck without trial."

In June before the election, Mosby, on an electioneering tour, encountered Benjamin Franklin Rixey at Vernon Mills. Rixey was no longer a state senator, but his Democratic gorge rose. After a sharp verbal exchange, the combatants set to, Rixey with his cane and Mosby with a buggy whip. No bones were broken, but the affray was reported gleefully by the Baltimore *Sun*, 15 June 1874, and attracted national attention.

Rixey had left the Virginia Senate in 1873 because affairs at home engaged his undivided attention. The restoration of *Vermont* to full production had been more difficult than he had expected. The fertility of the land had, itself, not been enough. Farm buildings had to be rebuilt, stock replenished, fences mended, equipment repaired or replaced and, above all, labor hired.

But it all took money!

Rixey began to borrow, not much at first, but in steadily increasing amounts. Newer and larger loans were needed to pay off the indebtedness on the old. The farms were producing, but not enough. The confidence of his creditors began to waiver. In February of 1878 the blow fell.

One of Benjamin F. Rixey's creditors died. The executor of his estate, a Loudoun County attorney, filed suit on behalf of the heirs of Robert C. Bowman and other creditors. Thus began the suit "Bowman's Executor vs. Rixey" which dragged through the court of chancery for twenty years.[9] The 2,199 acres of land was valued at $71,741 on 7 December 1878. The complicated arithmetic in the surviving papers is too tedious to record here, but it was soon evident that the liens against the property greatly exceeded its market value.

In 1878 Rixey was in robust health at age fifty-six. He had hoped to protect his creditors by, from time to time, taking out life insurance policies on which the premiums were staggering. The care and anxiety soon told on his physical strength. In March of 1881, when it became necessary to secure additional insurance, he had developed angina and no doctor would recommend him as an insurance risk. He had, long since, placed his property in his wife's name and, though she had joined in his notes, the fact that some of it was inherited from her father, raised a question of dower rights. In the summer of 1878 they made an effort to sell *Mountain View*, then called the *Morehead Farm*, but there were no takers. They needed something in the order of a miracle to save them.

The miracle arrived in the person of Colonel McKendree W. Jones. Colonel Jones is described in a sale brochure as "a New York gentleman of culture and refinement." More important, he had a wealthy wife. Mrs. Jones had to take but one look at *Vermont* to decide that she could not live in a "wooden house." Other reservations she may have had went unmentioned. On 10 August 1882, the Joneses bought the site of *Vermont* and 472 acres. Later they bought 143 additional acres from Rixey, making a total of 615 acres.

It was agreed that, if the Rixeys wanted to save the house and any of its outbuildings, they might do so if they were removed before the first of May, 1883. Benjamin Rixey barely made the deadline. Arming himself with a keg of "medicinal" whiskey, he ensconced himself in his house and the two set off down the road in the direction of Marshall.[10]

The site sold to Jones essentially included Henry Dixon's share of the dower land, most of which had been Lucius Dixon's share of the original division, bought from Shumate, and about 100 acres of the *Morehead Farm*. The new site of *Vermont* was Lucius Dixon's large wooded lot and much of the land west of it that had belonged to Alice (Dixon) Payne. It was still a fine farm of 586 acres.

With the sale of *Vermont* the Rixeys were far from being destitute. There was still over 1,500 acres of land, some of it no longer encumbered. It was about this time that the first bit of outwardly visible vandalism was committed on *Vermont*. Undoubtedly the original twelve light windows were mostly smashed during the move. They were replaced with ugly four-light sash which detracted from the scale of the house. The other "improvement" was more devastating still. Possibly emulating the Victorian gimcrackery being committed elsewhere, a pointed "Gothik" gable broke the serene roof line, complete with scrollwork and ending in a pointed spike. Both errors could easily have been remedied.

Before the eighteenth of April, 1885, Benjamin F. Rixey, broken in health and spirit, died at the age of sixty-three. Three years later a commission reported that the estate in the hands of executors had shrunk to 1,407 acres. Other than *Vermont* the best remaining land was the old Morehead home, now called the *White House*. Not long after her husband's

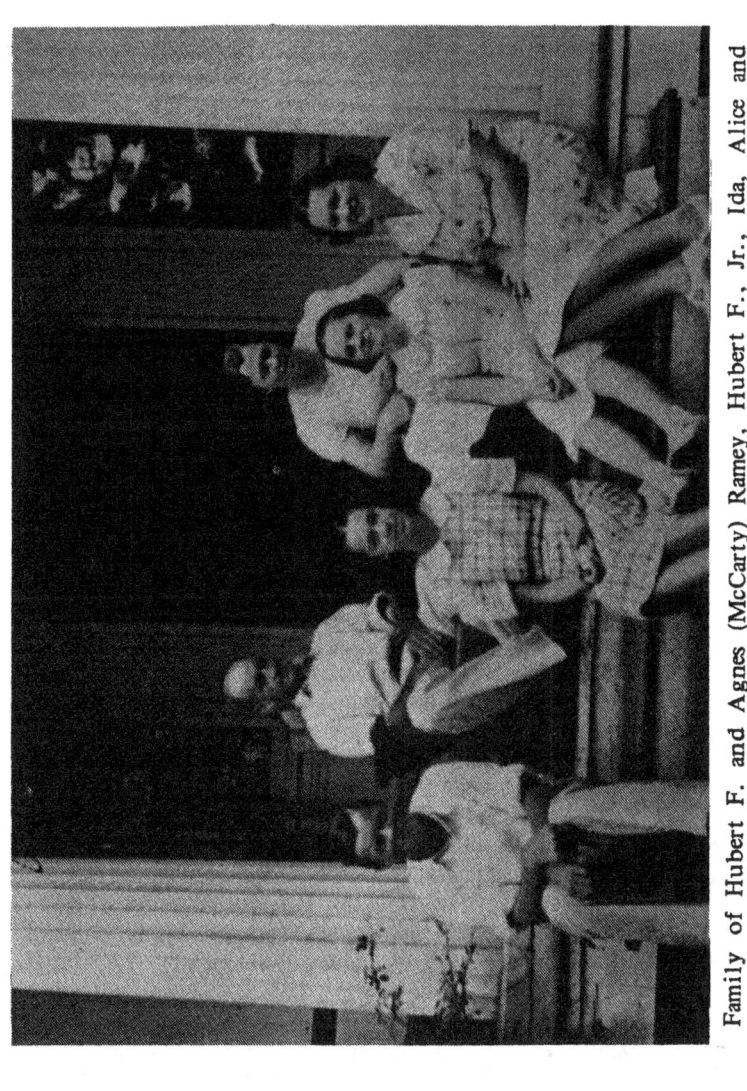

Family of Hubert F. and Agnes (McCarty) Ramey, Hubert F., Jr., Ida, Alice and Frances, seated on the porch at *Vermont*. Mr. Ramey was the manager of his uncle's (Charles F. Ramey) estate. --courtesy of Mrs. Alice R. Payne

death, Eleanora (Morehead) Rixey sold that land to J. William Miller.[11] The property then contained 379+ acres. Mrs. Rixey "having established her claim to a portion of the said land as her maiden property," received compensation. The rest of the purchase money was applied to the still-outstanding debts of the Rixey estate. Mr. Miller's granddaughter occupies the *White House* today.

The last of the Rixeys to live at *Vermont* were Miss Fanny and Miss Molly, spinster daughters of Benjamin F. and Eleanora (Morehead) Rixey. They sold it in 1902 and it passed through the hands of a series of owners, the last of whom had it torn down. It stood for at least 145 years, but nothing now remains of *Vermont* to remind us of its former glory.

GLENARA

If what was built on the site of *Vermont* was what Mrs. McKendree W. Jones had in mind, it is not difficult to understand why *Vermont* did not suit her. The building that began to evolve to the amazed awe of the local gentry was like nothing ever before seen in Fauquier County. It was mammoth. It was designed by a fashionable New York architect whose specialty was the execution of country places for rich New Yorkers in what he was pleased to call "the Italian style." Nothing remotely similar has ever been seen in Italy, and nothing more unsuitable to the Dixon Valley can be imagined. It was built of that particularly repulsive shade of plum-colored brick so dear to the Victorian heart and was dominated by an immense tower which made up in bulk what it lacked in grace. From the ground floor wide verandahs called piazzas were flung out in all directions, suffusing the rooms with a permanent gloom. As if that were not enough, these rooms were paneled in the darkest woods: ebony, teak, walnut and mahogany. When the paneling was not dark enough, it was stained to make it darker.[12]

No money was spared on its construction, no stone unturned. The water was analyzed and pronounced good for kidney disease and anything else that might be bothering you.[13] Flora and fauna abounded in the greatest profusion and of the most exotic species. The furnishings within were of almost stupefying elegance. Everywhere they were of the richest, darkest wood, upholstered in the heaviest, darkest material. The walls were hung with priceless oil paintings by no one knows whom, but the furnace was by Hyslop and the water closet (singular) was a masterpiece of J. L. Mott.

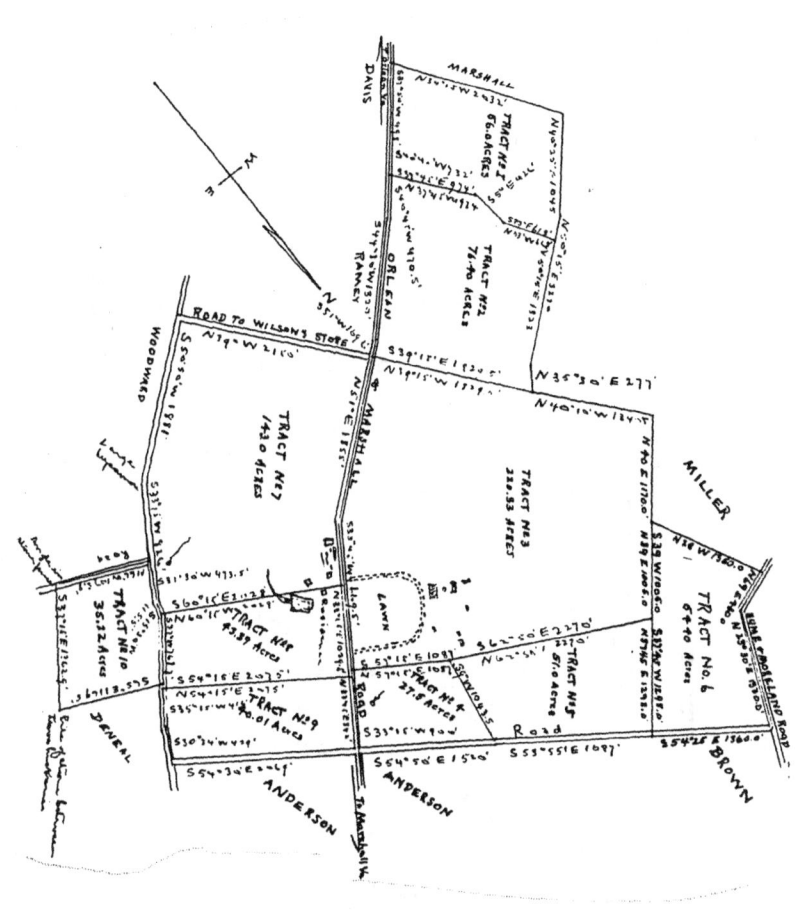

Subdivison of *Glenara*, 1922

--Fauquier Co. Deed 124, p. 187

"PROSPERITY"

HIGH PATENT
FLOUR

Made by Glenara Roller Mills
MARSHALL, VA.
J. B. SWANN, PROPRIETOR.

IN A CLASS BY ITSELF

This superior brand of flour is made from the finest quality of wheat obtainable in Northern Virginia. We supply the best trade throughout this section of the country, and we GUARANTEE SATISFACTION. Priced Reasonable   Local Orders Solicited.

D. F. DeButts, Traveling Salesman.

SATURDAY, SEPTEMBER 25 1909.

A GOOD REASON

nton People Can Tell You why It Is So.

Kidney Pills cure the sease, and that is why are always lasting. strengthens and kidneys, helping out of the body ns that cause e and distressurinary com- paople testi-

Water-
 says:
 Kidney
 bene-
 ived
 m.

Advertisement from *The Warrenton Virginian*, Warrenton, Va., for the product of the mill established by John Butler Swann, then owner of *Glenara*.

Glenara today. --courtesy of G. T. Ward

Glenara (ca. 1895). Probably pictured is Thomas Beck and his family, who owned the estate from 1891 to 1897. In 1897 Mr. Beck sold *Glenara* to John Morgan Davis, a scion of the *Vernon Mills* Davis family. Mr. Davis had discovered a silver lode in British Columbia and, according to his nephew, the late James Davis, mined $250,000 worth of ore from the Reco Mine by 1897. His brother, Henry Davis, of Marshall, moved his family to *Glenara*, where Mrs. Davis served as John M. Davis's hostess. After about nine years of lavish entertaining, the silver vein ran out and *Glenara* was sold to John Butler Swann.

--courtesy of G. T. Ward

As the Joneses stumbled through the Stygian blackness of the interior, they tripped over such miscellaneous bric-a-brac as a copy of the Farnese Bull found in the Baths of Caracalla, Persian rugs from the Vienna Exposition of 1877, and the royal coat-of-arms from Dresden. Some of the china was purchased in Paris and pronounced by Tiffany to be genuine (genuine what?). Greece, Egypt and the Holy Land had been ransacked for all their treasures. Mr. Tuthill had even designed the outbuildings, including, presumably, the hennery.

The Joneses christened all of this *Glenara* for a remote and ruined castle in the Scottish Highlands.

They visited it once in a while and owned it less than ten years. On 22 September 1891 Colonel Jones sold *Glenara* to Thomas Beck, lock, stock, barrel--and the Farnese Bull.[14] Thomas Beck's tenure was short lived. In 1897 he was offering to send his carriage to the station at Marshall to pick up prospective buyers. It is from his sales brochure on that occasion that we derive our intimate knowledge of the mansion's contents.[15] After several interim owners the most recent were sending automobiles to meet prospective buyers at a public auction of the house and land on the fifteenth of August, 1922. The size of the estate had grown from 615 acres to 865 acres by the addition from the remainder of Henry Dixon's land from the dower division and 117 acres of woodland three quarters of a mile away. The owners had subdivided the land and were prepared to sell it in ten separate parcels.[16]

In 1922 the house was little changed except that there were now five tiled baths to replace a single water closet. There is no mention of "elegant" furnishings, so they must have been removed to grace other rooms. Later and more tasteful owners have calmed *Glenara*'s Victorian exuberance. The "topless tower" is happily toppled. Shorn of its "piazzas," the sunlight penetrates the dark interior. It was then seen that, because of their very size, the rooms had a certain grandeur. Several healthy coats of white paint have covered the plum-colored brick. Among its stately trees *Glenara* is now at peace with its surroundings.

MOUNTAIN VIEW or THE WHITE HOUSE

Aside from *Vermont* and an overseer's house on the land later known as *Westwood*, the oldest house on the Turner Dixon grant belonged to John Morehead. The Moreheads had been in the area since long before the Dixons had moved there. The first John Morehead died in 1768, leaving a long and interesting will, naming six sons and three daughters. To his son John he left five shillings.

That did not bother Captain John Morehead who served with distinction in the Revolutionary War. Hardly was he out of the army than Turner Dixon's uncle complained that he was trespassing on his property in Fauquier.[17] Captain Morehead, who in the course of his military career had trespassed on a lot of property, was not disturbed by that either. Anyway, the old man died before he could press charges. Captain John Morehead died in 1821 leaving 11 children. One of these, John Morehead, bought 112.75 acres of Dixon's land between 1821 and 1833. The land doesn't appear on the 1821 survey of Turner Dixon's land; it does on the 1833 survey of the dower division.

On this exquisitely drawn survey, the tract is nearly square and, like Naboth's vineyard, is completely surrounded by the Dixon's land. It is described as adjoining the lands of James Keith Marshall on the north and the *Vermont* estate on the east and south, but Duncan's survey indicates that the frontage on the road from Salem to Hume was virtually nil. On 27 August 1835, John Morehead and his wife, Susannah (Humston) Morehead, conveyed this land to his brother Captain James Morehead. On the Duncan survey the house shown is modest, a single-storey frame building with one chimney. It is a considerable distance from the *White House* which later became the Morehead home. To this tract Captain James Morehead added bits and pieces of the Dixon tract as they became available: 123 acres from Turner Dixon in 1834, 17 acres from George Adams in 1838 that had been Charles Dixon's "small lot," and, in August 1838, all of Alice Dixon's 418.5 acres.[18]

Captain Morehead's first wife was a cousin, Ann Johnson, and by her he had four children: Armistead H., Eleanora, James Milton and DeWit Clinton Morehead. Before 1846 he married a second time. She was Frances Rixey, a lady who had a rather considerable property of her own. In the last year of his life Captain Morehead wrote, with almost complete disregard of accepted spelling or syntax, a number of memoranda in which he gave his wife various gifts, large and small. Mrs. Morehead was apparently embarrassed by these, hoping to recover after his death only the property that was hers before her marriage. Finally, in a prodigious outpouring of literary effort, she wrote a memorandum of her own:

> I Fany Morehead dwo not clame any
> part of my husbuns house hold furniture
> that he now has four beds.[19]

White House (ca. 1932). This house was built on part of the Turner Dixon grant purchased between 1821 and 1833 by John Morehead. In 1835 John Morehead conveyed the land to his brother, Captain James Morehead, who, it is thought, built the two-storey rubble-stone "L" shaped house. The property descended to Eleanora Morehead who married Benjamin F. Rixey and the property became involved with his estate. In 1893 it was purchased by J. William Miller and descended to his daughter, Sadie (Mrs. L. Lake Triplett); it is owned today by their daughter, Elise (Triplett) Mottley. --courtesy of Elise T. Mottley

Captain Morehead died before 22 February 1847. Two of his children were married by that time. Armistead H. Morehead married Eliza F. Rixey on 27 April 1840. On 7 January 1845, Eleanora Morehead married Benjamin F. Rixey. Shortly after his father's death, James Milton Morehead married Elizabeth W. Hunter. It is pleasant to report that Frances (Rixey) Morehead got all that she wanted, her personal property and her rocking chair.[20]

Captain James Morehead owned a considerable amount of property not necessarily contiguous to *Mountain View*, as his place was called. Even before he bought *Mountain View*, he had bought 34 acres with a mill upon it from the estate of William Dixon, deceased. The mill was, of course, on Thumb Run. Below it he built a better mill so that, when he died, there was an Upper Mill valued at $400 and a Lower Mill valued at $2,000. The value of his entire estate was set at $23,103.25, a large estate for the time.

A valiant attempt was made to divide this odd-shaped piece of real estate equally between Captain Morehead's four children.[21]

Eleanora Rixey received 119 acres of cleared land at the south end, 37 acres of woodland at the extreme north end where all the wooded land was, the Upper Mill and half the Lower Mill.

Armistead H. Morehead received *Mountain View* with 101 acres of cleared land, 42 acres of woodland and the duty of paying his sister and brother, DeWit Clinton Morehead, for the slightly greater value of his share.

James Milton Morehead received 134 acres of cleared land, 37 acres of woodland and the other half of the Lower Mill. He placed his inheritance, on which there was no dwelling, temporarily in the hands of his brother, Armistead, and may have left the Dixon Valley for a short time.

DeWit Clinton Morehead (no effort was ever made to spell the name of the American statesman, De Witt Clinton, correctly), received 164 acres of cleared land at the north end and 37 acres of woodland. It is the only instance where the cleared land and the woodland were contiguous.

It was stated additionally that there was uncertainty as to the location of the line between the estate and the Rogers' *Vermont*. Any loss accruing from that fact was to be borne equally by all parties. The division was made by James Keith Marshall, John Shumate and George Adams. It was dated 9 October 1848.[22]

Armistead H. Morehead arranged the sale of his and his brother's land to Benjamin F. Rixey on 20 March 1852.[23] The deed mentions 390 acres, but 88 of these acres he had previously bought from his sister, Eleanora Rixey, and was selling them back. For James Milton Morehead, it was really only an exchange of property. Four days previously he had bought *Bleak House* from Benjamin F. Rixey.[24]

The deed from DeWit Clinton Morehead to Benjamin F. Rixey for his 201 acres has not been found but he, too, apparently left the Dixon Valley. The Morehead name continued in Fauquier County for several generations thereafter, so it appears that one or more of the brothers lived elsewhere in the county. Their lives at *Mountain View* had, however, ended. The further history of that beautiful estate was caught up in the tangled affairs of Benjamin F. Rixey.

EASTWOOD

The property known as *Eastwood* was the home of Mary Jane (Dixon) Scott until her death in 1833.[25] It contained 254 acres from the original division of the Turner Dixon estate, and an additional 105 acres from her mother's dower division of 1833. To this was added, before 1850, an irregularly shaped tract of 35 acres across the Salem-Orlean Road and outside the original grant. This land was, of course, held in trust for her four children, Robert Scott, Turner Dixon Scott, Marianna Scott and William Dixon Scott, until they should come of age. When the property was divided in 1850 Robert Scott was given 95.5 acres; Turner D. Scott the manor house and another 95.5 acres; Marianna Scott 98.5 acres; and William D. Scott 104.5 acres.[26]

It appears that Turner D. Scott sold his share to his brother Robert, having already bought land from Lucius Dixon, as previously mentioned. On 6 May 1851, William D. Scott sold his portion of the farm to John Shumate.[27] Then, on 10 March 1853, Shumate bought Marianna Scott's 98.5 acres, plus 4 acres she had purchased from her brother Robert.[28] He also bought a little more than 2 acres from Robert Scott, 16 February 1852.[29] This gave Shumate 209 acres of the 394-acre *Eastwood* property available when the division between the Dixon heirs was made.

The plat, made by George W. Norris, April 1850, shows that the land bought by John Shumate was the eastern half, lying on both sides of the Salem-Orlean Road, an area most of which was later known as the Frazier Farm. Apparently, John Shumate also acquired the remaining 185 acres, including the manor house at *Eastwood* from Robert Scott soon after. This he promptly sold to Benjamin F. Rixey, who was in the midst of his land-buying spree just before the war. After the war began, feeling the need for some retrenchment, Rixey sold the 190 acres to John T. Jones.[30]

John T. Jones was acting as the executor of the estate of his brother, William R. Jones, who had died in 1859. William R. Jones had been Rixey's brother-in-law, having married Alice P. Rixey, daughter of Samuel Rixey, Sr. In his will, dated 2/14/1859, William R. Jones rather gracelessly excluded his wife from her dower rights on the ground that she had received enough from her father. That was probably true, as Samuel Rixey, Sr. had also settled $10,000 each on their two children, Mary Fendall and William Turner Jones. He named his brother, John T. Jones, executor with instructions to invest his estate "in real or personal property as might seem best and most secure," for the benefit of his children. John T. Jones did so, buying *Eastwood* next to their home, the Andrew Barbee estate, called *Cleveland*, for his young wards. He also invested in slaves required to maintain these properties. He had not, unfortunately, reckoned with the consequences of the war.

The solvency of his brother's estate depended heavily on the value of his slaves. When that asset was removed, and the ravages of war were taken into account, the estate was unable to meet the obligations contracted by its executor. Benjamin F. Rixey sued for the unpaid balance due on *Eastwood*, thereby encouraging other creditors to file claims. The court ordered the property sold at public auction, 24 August 1868.[31]

The highest bidder was Charles T. Brown, who agreed to pay $9,000 over a term of years. Charles Thornton Brown (1822-1885) was a son of John and Matilda (Christie) Brown of Fauquier County. On 23 September 1846 he married Mary Ann Jeffries, daughter of George and Sally (Welch) Jeffries. In the years that followed, Brown had difficulty meeting the payments because of the depressed economy that reigned during that period in the South. However, by 13 May 1881, he had made all the payments and was given title to the property.[32]

The Brown Place, now called *Valley Dale Farm*, remained in the possession of Charles T. Brown's descendants until 1956, when it was sold by the heirs of his son, Moses J. Brown, to Victor and Rosa (Rector) Hacker.[33] The original house at *Eastwood* no longer exists. The comfortable house on the property is of a later period, and none of the present outbuildings date from that time except, possibly, part at least of a small structure, known as the Lower House, which may have been one of its dependencies.

Eastwood (The Brown Place). The building is thought to have existed during the Alexander B. Scott ownership. In the 19th century it was known as the Lower House and was probably servants' quarters or an outside kitchen. It contains one ground-floor room and one above reached by a stairway. --courtesy Barbara (Brown) Searles

Eastwood (The Brown Place), ca. 1915. Pictured are Moses Jackson Brown and wife, Mary Jane (Mollie) Wines Brown, in swing. ---courtesy of Barbara (Brown) Searles

Chimney at the site of *Eastwood*, home of Alexander Brown Scott and his wife, Mary Jane (Dixon) Scott. Located near Ada, Virginia. --courtesy of Barbara (Brown) Searles

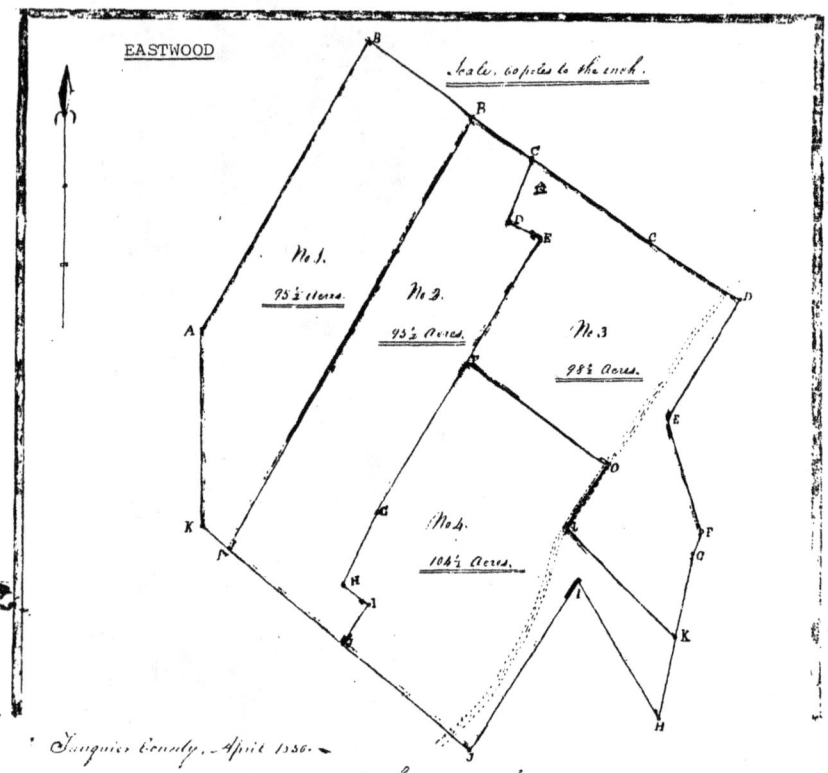

Fauquier County, April 1836.—

At the request of the Commissioners appointed by said to divide the land of Alexander B. Veell among his children, I surveyed the land above represented, Beginning at A, a stake S. W. of a Hickory and running with W. Slow and Spon. N 57½ E 170½ p. to B, thence with Hedon S 57 E. 180 p. to C, a stake, thence S 22½ E. 55 p. to D, a stone, thence S 27 W 22 p. to E, a Chesnut, thence S 27 E. 54½ p. to F, a Red oak, thence S 65 W 112 p. to G, a Red Oak, thence S 11 W 24 p. to H, a Chesnut, thence N 33 W 33 p. to I, a pile of stones, thence S 29 W 112 p. to J, a stone, thence N 54 W 178 p. to K, a stone between two Red Oaks, thence N 34 W 12 p. to the Beginning, Containing three hundred and ninety four acres.

Charles Thornton Brown
1821-1885

Purchased *Eastwood* in 1868, which was to be the Brown family home for eighty-five years.

--courtesy of Barbara (Brown) Searles

Moses Jackson Brown
1851-1927

Son of Charles Thornton Brown and Mary Ann (Jeffries) Brown. He inherited *Eastwood* from his father who died in 1885.

--courtesy of Barbara (Brown) Searles

Henry Edwin Brown
1894 - 1952

Son of Moses J. and Mary Jane Brown. Henry E. Brown and his family were the last of the Brown family to farm *Eastwood*.

--courtesy of Barbara (Brown) Searles

Charles Hampton Brown, Sr.
1899 - 1990

Son of Moses J. and Mary Jane (Wines) Brown

--courtesy of Barbara (Brown) Searles

However, on a nearby hill is a lonely chimney flanked by two old trees. The former owners believed that this was part of a tenant house, but its location in relation to the original boundary of *Eastwood* and the obvious advantages of the site make it highly probable that it was part of the old mansion. We know that the original house stood quite close to the southern boundary of the first dividend of 254 acres, so much so, in fact, that to protect, it Mary Jane (Dixon) Scott was persuaded (unnecessarily as it turned out) to purchase nine acres from her brother, George B. Dixon, in 1831. The old chimney is very close to the line and the so-called Lower House is also. One can well understand her anxiety.

It also argues that the original house was built before the first division of the Dixon lands, as it is unlikely that anyone would have built a house so close to a boundary, had that boundary been predetermined. It is probable that *Eastwood* was unoccupied during the war and thus prey to marauding troops.

It is impossible to state positively that the site of *Eastwood* has been found, but the present owners might be tempted to dig around the old chimney in search of artifacts to prove one way or another.

WESTWOOD

Thomas Lawrence Maddux was the son of Thomas Maddux who had for many years kept an "ordinary at his house at Fauquier Courthouse." Although the ordinary had been reasonably respectable, the younger Maddux wondered whether or not it provided the right atmosphere in which to raise a large family. In 1835, when he bought George Beverley Dixon's share of his father's grant in the Dixon Valley called *Westwood*, he had already been married for more than twenty years and had eleven of his children, six sons and five daughters.[34] Two more sons, by far the most colorful of the lot, were to be born at *Westwood*. His decision to try farming was a happy one, but did not eradicate from his children that talent for innkeeping, to which several of them eventually returned.[35]

The house he built for his family at *Westwood* was a small, sturdy, two-storey stone structure of simple design. It still stands, attractively restored in its grove of ancient trees. Adjacent to it was built a log structure that served as the kitchen. Of this, only a stone chimney remains. Between the house and cemetery he erected a two-storey barracks-like building which served as a dormitory for his eight sons. This building has long since fallen. Mr. Maddux tackled the life of a farmer with enthusiasm, and a list of his farm equipment, made after his death, is indicative of what was needed at that time to operate a small farm. For *Westwood*'s 225 acres, a figure that remained constant for more than one hundred years, was small for an estate of the period. It was adequate to support the Maddux family but not to provide a useful homestead for thirteen children, or even his eight sons. Thomas L. Maddux realized this and wrote his will accordingly.

Unfortunately Thomas Maddux died after only four years at his new farm. His will, dated 3 July 1839, was submitted to probate 26 August of the same year. He was buried in the family burying ground at *Westwood*.[36] It is recorded that his funeral cost thirty dollars and his tombstone sixteen. His will is a model of clarity, if not of wisdom. However, clairvoyance cannot be expected of the dead.[37]

In the will, Dorcas (Davis) Maddux, his wife, was asked to play a somewhat ambiguous role. She was given the use of the land until her youngest child should come of age (1859), after which it was to be sold and the proceeds divided among his heirs, "she taking a child's share." However, he gave her discretionary power to sell the land if she should elect to move to "the Western Country" and re-invest the money in western land. Unaccountably he gave his daughter Maria Louisa a riding horse, "as the care and support of my youngest children will naturally devolve upon her." At that time Maria Louisa Maddux was only six years old. The only possible explanation is that Dorcas Maddux was his second wife and Maria Louisa the eldest of her children. He does provide that his son, William D. Maddux, then age twenty-five, should take charge of the younger children in the event of his wife's death. The sale of his property when his youngest child should come of age makes no special provision for his Negroes. They were to be sold along with the rest of his personal property.

Dorcas Maddux had no intention or desire to move West, but she seized upon that clause in the will to authorize sale of the property at public auction in 1851, when her youngest son was only thirteen years old. She had not thought of the fate of her unfortunate slaves and, when she realized that they, too, would be sold, she attended the sale and made an impassioned plea that she be allowed to buy them, not for herself but for the benefit of her late husband's estate and the benefit of his children. No gentleman would bid against her and she got them, as was later alleged, at an absurdly low price. After the sale she considered the Negroes as being exclusively her own property,

Westwood. Sold to Thomas L. Maddux by George B. Dixon, 1835. The portion between the stone house and chimney was built of log. There was another house in the yard where the Maddux sons slept. --photo by author, 1978

to dispose of as she saw fit, in clear violation of the intent of her deceased husband.[38]

Though Dorcas Maddux may not have had the law on her side, her heart was certainly in the right place. She only wanted to leave the Negroes to her and her husband's daughters, not the sons. There were only seven of them, probably all of the same family. Old Nace, the only one mentioned in Thomas L. Maddux's will, was apparently too old to work. There was a man named Ennis, who was in poor health. The most valuable was Hannah, who had an infant child. The rest, a boy named Bushrod, and two girls, Frances and Ellen, were children. When Dorcas Maddux made her will, 4 March 1853, the two oldest Maddux girls were married. Margaret, the eldest, had married Silas J. Saunders just before her father's death. Mary Evaline had married Jacob Heflebower, proprietor of the City Hotel (once Gadsby's Tavern) in Alexandria. In 1855 Silas J. and Margaret (Maddux) Saunders were also living in Alexandria. Dorcas Maddux gave them the two Negroes best able to endure separation from the family, Ennis to Margaret Saunders and Bushrod to Mary Heflebower. Between the three unmarried daughters, Jane Elizabeth, 24, Caroline Virginia, 22, and Maria Louisa, 20, she left $1,000 in cash left by her husband, which she had not touched, each a bed and furniture, and her carriage to be used jointly but ultimately to belong to the last one married. Hannah, her child, and the two girls, Fanny and Ellen, were to remain with the sisters. The will was carefully thought out and eminently reasonable. It is a pity that the older Maddux boys did not see it that way.

The flowers on Dorcas Maddux's grave had barely wilted when the six oldest Maddux sons filed suit to break her will. They sued, of course, Silas J. Saunders, administrator of her estate. That unfortunate man may have repented marrying into the Maddux family, as most of his married life was spent in litigation relating to its affairs. George W. Maddux was apparently the aggressor. William D. Maddux, although he joined in the suit, washed his hands of the whole thing and, to his credit, assigned the proceeds to his wife and children. The two youngest boys, Thomas Clay Maddux and Franklin Webster Maddux, were represented by their guardian. One of the three younger girls was married, Caroline Virginia Maddux having married Wesley D. Miller shortly after her mother's death. They lived in Clarke County.

The court had very little discretion in the matter. The will of Thomas Lawrence Maddux was clear enough, though he had not anticipated the circumstances. The property was ordered sold. George W. Maddux bought most of it as well as

Hannah and her child, Ellen, and most of the furniture of *Westwood*. He did accept the care of Old Nace. Saunders bought the two children, Bushrod and Fanny, and Martin van Buren Maddux, the sixth son, took Ennis. Wesley D. Miller tried to buy *Westwood* but was unable to raise funds, so he transferred the purchase to Margaret (Maddux) Saunders. This gave rise to another lawsuit.[39]

One Zephaniah Turner filed suit against Saunders and the entire Maddux family for five percent commission on the sale of *Westwood* originally agreed upon by Wesley D. Miller. Saunders answered quite logically that he did not owe the commission, since he had been quietly buying up the shares of the thirteen heirs and already owned eight of them in addition to the one to which he was entitled in the right of his wife. The Maddux heirs had scattered by that time. Alfred and Edward had deeded theirs to their mother before her death and Saunders had obtained them from her. On 29 January 1852, George W. Maddux had sold him his share and also those of James H. and Martin V. Maddux, which he had purchased. Subsequently, he had acquired the shares of Caroline (Maddux) Miller, Mary (Maddux) Heflebower and, finally on 18 September 1857, that of Thomas Clay Maddux. Saunders was willing to pay a commission on the remaining four shares, amounting to $155, not the $506 claimed by Turner. This time Saunders won.

Silas J. Saunders and his wife lived at *Westwood* until his death. In May 1872, Alfred Maddux, trustee of Margaret (Maddux) Saunders, finally settled the last claim.[40] Silas J. and Margaret (Maddux) Saunders had no children and *Westwood* became the property of Franklin Webster (F. Webb) Maddux, last surviving son of Thomas Lawrence and Dorcas (Davis) Maddux. Dr. Thomas Clay Maddux, who became famous because of his quarrel with Henry Dixon, had died in 1881. F. Webb Maddux lived at *Oak Hill*. When he died in 1905 he left *Westwood* to his second daughter, Kitty Lee Maddux, wife of Evan Warfield Hook of Baltimore, Maryland. In July 1913, Mrs. Hook sold the property to Frederick W. and Pauline (Platt) Okie, owners of *Cleveland*.[41] In September 1918, Mrs. Okie sold it to James M. Curtis, who kept it until 1924.[42] He sold it to John T. Ramey.[43] It has since remained in the Ramey family except the house and about 22 acres around it. The present owners are carefully restoring the "manor of Westwood," now nearly 150 years old.[44]

SILVER SPRING

Unlike its nearest neighbors, *Silver Spring* has a history largely free of the litigation that has beset them in the last 150 years. It lies just north of the center of Turner Dixon's original grant. In the division of his estate made in 1821, it fell to his son, John Dixon, then seven years old. It contained 315 acres to which was added, in 1833, a woodland strip of 23.5 acres from the division of his mother's dower land. As John Dixon was never mentally competent to handle his estate, it was rented for him by his guardian, Peter Adams. In 1843 John Dixon died at the age of twenty-nine.[45]

Robert E. Scott and Samuel Chilton, acting as commissioners in the lawsuit over the estate of Maria Dixon, conveyed his tract, less about ten acres lost in minor boundary adjustment, to Dr. Thomas Thornton Withers in October of 1844.[46] Dr. Withers was then in his forties. He was a son of Enoch Keene and Janette (Chinn) Withers of *Green Meadows*, Fauquier County. He had never married and lived there, presumably alone, in a modest, pleasantly proportioned house to which some unfortunate additions were made in later years. He was too old to take active part in the war that was soon to come, but he suffered, as did his neighbors, endless raids upon his livestock and grain supply by armies of both sides. Then, as the stillness at Appomattox descended in April of 1865, Dr. Withers died as he lived, quietly.[47]

His executor, John A. Spilman, offered *Silver Spring* to public auction 3 May 1865. The highest bidder was John T. Jones, at $6,012, but Jones was not acting for himself. He quickly sold the land to John William Hunter Rixey and his brother, Benjamin F. Rixey. John H. Rixey took 299 acres and Benjamin F. Rixey 35 acres. Six acres of the original 338.5 acres had, somehow, been recovered.[48]

Unfortunately John W. Hunter Rixey lived to enjoy *Silver Spring* only four years after it was deeded to him, 29 November 1871. It was soon back on the market, 299 acres and an additional 17 acres picked up along its border, for a total of 316 acres. This was sold in 1882 to Mrs. "Jeannie S. Jones."[49] Mrs. Jones was Jane S. McGuire of Fauquier County, daughter of Robert Lewis and Agnes (Douthat) McGuire. She had married James Fitzgerald Jones, of a distinguished Fauquier family. His father, James Fitzgerald Jones, Sr., had married, 2 January 1845, Anne Lewis Marshall, daughter of Thomas and Margaret Wardrop (Lewis) Marshall and granddaughter of Chief Justice John Marshall. In the division of the estate of Thomas

In 1836 Peter Adams, guardian of John Dixon, paid Joseph H. Robinson $175.00 for building "a house on John Dixon's land." Since the Curtis family ownership (1968), this house on *Silver Spring* has fallen into disrepair. --photo by the author, 1978

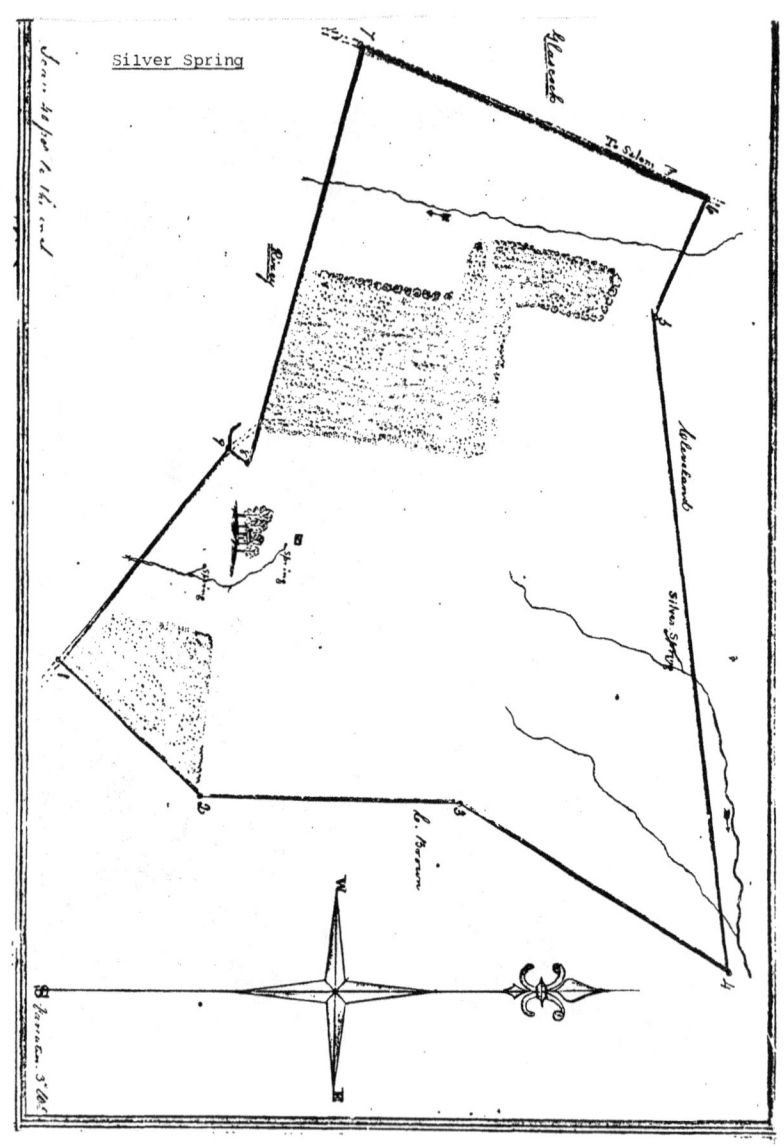

Marshall, Anne (Marshall) Jones had received *Woodside*, part of the *Oak Hill* estate.

James Fitzgerald Jones, Jr., was born at *Woodside* 27 July 1853. As a young man he was employed by the United States Bureau of Internal Revenue, which was, in those dear, dead, uncomplicated days, a minor branch of the Department of Interior. His duties consisted chiefly of checking the activities of moonshiners in the Blue Ridge Mountains and elsewhere--maybe even closer to home! He survived this onerous assignment which, according to his obituary, "involved no slight personal risk." He loved his Dixon Valley home where he and his wife had four children, one of whom died in childhood.[50]

To buy *Silver Spring* Mr. Jones borrowed about half the purchase price, $3000, from his sister, Frances Barton Jones, and a lesser amount, $1,156, of H. Clay Bayley. These amounts were still outstanding when, on 21 May 1887, "Jeanie" Jones died, leaving no estate other than this encumbered land. However, because *Silver Spring* was in his wife's name, the previous owners were obliged to deed the property to her surviving children, Robert M. Jones, William S. Jones, and James Fitzgerald Jones, III, which they did 25 February 1891.[51]

In order to pay off the indebtedness on the place James F. Jones had found a purchaser for more than 89 acres at the west side of the property which was surveyed 22 January 1891. The buyer was John H. Lee, who owned the adjoining property called *Moreland*. It thus became a part of *Moreland* as we will see later.[52]

James F. Jones and his children continued to live at *Silver Spring*. He married his deceased wife's sister, Mary Anna Carter McGuire, called Minna. Having served with the Bureau of Internal Revenue long enough, exposing himself to the risks involved, he decided to retire in 1902. He had bought a place called *Hilton* in King George County, where he had been asked to take over the management of the immense *Caledon Farm*. He filed a friendly suit against his children, with their consent, to recoup the amounts of money paid out by him to keep their estate together.[53] On the first of January, 1903, *Silver Spring* was sold to J. M. Curtis.[54] William N. Curtis, a son and one of the heirs of James M. Curtis, became the next owner of *Silver Spring*.[55] After being in the Curtis family for sixty-five years, the farm was sold by Mrs. Nannie Hall Curtis, widow of W. N. Curtis, to William H. Leachman Jr.[56]

BLEAK HOUSE

On 27 December 1843, Lucius Dixon sold all of the land he had inherited from his father's estate. About half of it, a total of 235 acres, he sold to his 19-year-old nephew, Turner Dixon Scott, for $4,700. Four years later, as the affairs of Lucius Dixon approached a dreadful climax, young Scott had been able to pay only a token amount of his indebtedness. Most of the land was in a tract of 166 acres west of the Salem-Orlean Grade Road adjoining *Vermont*. In addition there was 40 acres of woodland along the same road adjoining land recently bought by John Shumate and a small lot of 28 acres corner to Charles C. Dixon's dividend. It was a beautiful property and Scott would probably have liked to have held on to it, but it was beginning to look as though anyone who owed money to the Lucius Dixon estate would be badly hurt. Accordingly, on 7 January 1850 he sold the whole property to Benjamin F. Rixey.[57]

In a deed dated 16 March 1852, Benjamin F. Rixey described the 166-acre *Bleak House* property as the "Farm on which the said Rixey now lives." That would appear to date the construction of the present house, which was certainly not built by Turner Dixon Scott. To the estate was added 307.75 acres across the Grade Road, part of a larger tract he had split with his cousin, Smith H. Rixey.[58]

The house is an interesting one. Today it is but a sad reminder of what it was in its heyday. The plan is an unusual one, departing sharply from the center-hall plan familiar to builders of an earlier period. The exterior was in a sophisticated Greek Revival style with a deeply recessed entrance porch and beautifully proportioned openings. Crowning the whole was a deep frieze in a wall-of-Troy motif, picked out in brilliantly contrasting colors, as were the capitals of the Doric columns and the triglyphs of the delicate frieze above them. The whole effect was one of elegance and refinement suitable to a young man of wealth and culture.

The source of the name *Bleak House* is, of course, no mystery. In 1852 Charles Dickens' novel with that title was reaching America in monthly installments to steadily mounting excitement. Nothing less like the Bleak House of Dickens' imagining than this house in the Virginia piedmont is conceivable, but the name was fashionably literary in tone and no one knew how the novel would turn out anyway.

The house was not a large one and Benjamin F. Rixey did not live there long. When the time came to trade it with

Bleak House, ca. 1900. Seated: Landonia (Lake) Skinner, widow of Benjamin F. Skinner, and her sons and daughters (unidentified). --author's collection

Bleak House --photo by the author, 1978

his brother-in-law, James Milton Morehead, for the latter's share of the Morehead estate, he did so without great reluctance.

There is a sharp demarcation between the printed history of *Bleak House* and the facts revealed by a title search. It is stated flatly that the house was built about 1830 by Samuel Rixey on a plan similar to other Rixey houses.[59] Samuel Rixey never owned the property or built, as far as is known, a house like it. It is said to have been occupied during the war years 1861 to 1865 by Sampson P. Bayly and his family, and a pretty story is told of a trap door in the floor of the downstairs bedroom through which the Bayly plate was concealed during raids by Yankee troops.

One hates to destroy romance by citing cold fact, but the record shows that James Milton Morehead (whose wife was not a Rixey as stated, but Elizabeth W. Hunton) deeded the property on 27 April 1863 to Silas J. Saunders, acting as trustee of Jane F. Maddux, wife of James H. Maddux, and her children. Possibly the Baylys rented the house at some time during that period but they did not own it. After the war Silas J. Saunders, acting still on behalf of the Madduxes, sold *Bleak House* to Robert G. Violett. On 5 March 1869, the whole story is recited in a deed to Violett in which it is pointed out that the surveys in the previous deeds had all been inaccurate. This deed was presumably to reassure Robert Violett that the property he had bought had some fixed boundaries, however difficult it had been to locate them.[60]

Three months later, Robert G. Violett and Amanda M., his wife, of Alexandria, sold the four hundred acres on both sides of the graded road adjoining Benjamin F. Rixey, Gray Carroll, Joseph B. Smith and others to Benjamin F. Skinner.[61] After this conveyance the printed history is more easily reconciled with fact. The house remained in the Skinner family until 1905, when it was sold by the heirs to Charles F. Ramey who married Lucy Skinner. A photograph of the house taken 1900 with an elegant and charmingly grouped family in front of it is a period piece that convincingly transmits the flavor of a bygone time.

THE SHUMATE PLACE

On Friday, 17 October 1766, there appeared in the *Maryland Gazette* a curious item:

> Died in Fauquier County, Virginia, John de la Shumat, age 130. Banished from France in 1684, he was imported to Virginia to settle Brent Town lands. He was a great-great-grandfather.

He was Jean de la Chaumette and he was not 130 years old, but he was very old indeed. Born in France about 1663, he was obliged to flee as a result of the revocation of the Edit of Nantes in 1685. By the thousands, French Protestants left France when this last hope of freedom to practice their religion was ruthlessly ended by Louis XIV. Many sought refuge in England and ultimately came to Virginia. In 1687 Nicholas Hayward, a London merchant, was advertising for settlers for the tract of land granted by Lord Culpeper to Richard Foote, his brother-in-law; Robert Bristow; George Brent; and himself. The Brent Town tract was 30,000 acres in the backwoods of Stafford County in the fork between Broad and Cedar Runs and extending to the back line in what is now Fauquier County. The project was a failure owing largely to its proximity to the Iroquois Hunting Path and consequent danger of attack by Indians. Nevertheless Jean de la Chaumette may well have been one of the earliest settlers in what is now Fauquier County.

Jean de la Chaumette was a great-great-grandfather, but, in 1766, the man we know as John Shumate was as yet unborn. However, he was one of those great-great-grand children. If Jean de la Chaumette had really lived to be 130 years old he would have witnessed John's birth in 1792. He was probably a son of Thomas and Mary (Dodson) Shumate who lived in the neighborhood of Elk Run.[62]

John Shumate made his first appearance in the records of the Dixon Valley at the age of thirty-six when he bought Henry Thomas Dixon's 254-acre share of the original division of his father's land.[63] On this land he lived the remainder of his life. His house was a simple one long since destroyed. Another house has been built on the same site on a bend in the road from Salem to Orlean. He had no taste for romantic names. It was always known simply as the *Shumate Place*. The distinction he gave it was not in its name but in its careful

88

John Shumate
1795-1872

Large landowner and prominent farmer of Dixon's Valley.

--courtesy of the late Mrs. Mildred (Ford) Prettyman

cultivation. John Shumate was one of the best farmers in Fauquier County, a shrewd appraiser of land, an excellent judge of horses and cattle, and a reliable advisor on farm management. He was a man of no great culture, fair education and, above all, absolute probity. He was much esteemed by his friends and neighbors for his sound judgment and integrity. Whenever there was an estate to be settled that involved property division, one of those chosen to act was John Shumate. Then each of the heirs could count on receiving an equitable share, both in quantity and in quality.

Little by little in the years following the purchase of his first land in the Dixon Valley from Henry T. Dixon in 1828, John Shumate increased his holdings. In 1832 he added 24 acres, 1 rood (1/4 acre) and 25 poles from George Beverley Dixon.[64] This was land that Dixon had bought from his brother, Turner Dixon, and adjoined Shumate's land on the south. In 1839 he bought 93.75 acres from Alexander Dixon.[65] This land was east of the road from Salem to Orlean and was part of the tract Alexander Dixon received in the first division of his father's estate. The remainder he sold to Marshall Jett. This tract was too small and too far removed from John Shumate's home place to be of much value. It was sold before his death.

In November 1843 John Shumate bought another detached property of much greater size. It comprised 223.5 acres of Lucius Dixon's share of the first division of his father's land, 19.5 acres of woodland and 2 acres of a smaller tract that Lucius Dixon owned, a total of 245 acres.[66] In reality, though, he found the operation of two separate farms impractical and, when the opportunity arose in 1863, he sold all of this land to Benjamin F. Rixey. It adjoined *Vermont* and became part of that estate.

Closer to home and therefore much more desirable was *Eastwood*, formerly the home of Mary Jane (Dixon) Scott. It was parceled out among her four children after her death in 1833 and, after they came of age between 1851 and 1853, John Shumate picked up William Dixon Scott's 104.5 acres and Marianna T. Scott's 98.5 acres plus 4 acres she had bought from her brother Robert. He also bought a little more than 2 acres directly from Robert Scott. The whole amounted to about 208.5 acres.[67]

This was the next to the last addition to the *Shumate Place*. Just before his death he commissioned R. T. Scott to secure for him 55 acres from the estate of Samuel Bayley who owned *Grafton*, the estate immediately north of the Turner Dixon grant.[68] It was considered part of *Grafton* though it was across the road. It had been part of Turner Dixon's dividend from the original division of his father's estate. Turner Dixon had sold it to his brother George B. Dixon, who conveyed it to Bayley as part of a larger tract, 26 October 1835. It was poor land and it is difficult to understand why Shumate wanted it unless it was needed to consolidate the boundaries of his property. He died before he had a chance to bring it up to the standard he set for all his property.

However, John Shumate did buy one other property, across the Salem-Orlean Road (The Graded Road) opposite the *Shumate Place*. It had contained 102.5 acres, but part of it was lost by a slight alteration of the road, so that there were only about 100 acres when he died. He bought it 24 May 1861 from Miss Jane Smith.[69] It is not necessary here to go into the long, tedious detail of the chancery suit that had resulted in this particular piece of property having fallen to three spinster Smith sisters, of whom Miss Jane was the last survivor. On the property there was a dilapidated house and the entire place had suffered from years of neglect. For John Shumate, though, it served a very special purpose.[70]

John Shumate never married. When he was quite advanced in years he formed a permanent liaison with his housekeeper, Catherine Gaines, described in his will as a "free born person of color now living with me." She bore him four children, a son Taylor Scott, and three daughters, Sarah Catherine, Adelaide Elizabeth, and Nancy Mason. These are the cold facts. The story behind them is an interesting commentary on the legal and moral atmosphere that prevailed in the South at that time and for a long time thereafter.

Catherine Gaines was devoted to John Shumate as only a gentle and affectionate woman could be. He, in turn, was grateful, kind and considerate. He promised her that, when he died, she and her children would be comfortably provided for. With every ounce of his failing strength, he endeavored to do just that. The result only proves that the dead, from their graves, cannot control the acts of the living, and that friends are not always what they seem.

His will, written and rewritten many times, was drawn with full realization of the legal climate in which his wishes would be carried out. Catherine Gaines was illiterate and it would have been disastrous to have given her a share in the management of his estate or to leave it to her outright. There was a nephew, the heir-at-law, waiting in the wings, ready, willing and able to break the will if he made such a move. Furthermore, even if the nephew was unsuccessful, there were many to take advantage of her, with whom she was unprepared to cope. His son, Taylor Scott Shumate alias Gaines still underage, intelligent, proud, but with no taste for book-learning. His daughters thirsted for knowledge he knew they must have if they were to make their way in a hostile world. Catherine Gaines, herself, was only too aware of her limitations and wanted more for her children than she had had.

John Shumate's plan was simple. The Smith house, untenanted since its purchase in 1861, could be repaired and made comfortable for Kitty (Catherine) Gaines and her children. The land was to be theirs to farm and to raise the turkeys, hens and potatoes, as she had always done for extra money to buy little luxuries. John Shumate believed in work but he believed just as firmly that work should bring its just reward. He never intended that they be supported on the proceeds of his little farm. His children were too young and the potential too limited to make that possible.

Instead he instructed his executors to rent the *Shumate Place* to a substantial and reliable farmer for as much as it would bring, under bond to keep it in good repair, the fences mended and the soil diligently restored. From this rental he expected funds ample enough to keep Kitty Gaines in comfortable circumstances and to educate his children to whatever degree their natural intelligence made possible. He also wanted provisions made so that when his children were all of age and had completed their education they would be given the option of living on the farm. In addition, Shumate planned to insure that executors would sell the farm and divide the proceeds among his children's heirs after the death of his last surviving child.

There was no legal way to do this other than to ask two of his friends to serve as executors and trustees, who could be relied upon to take good care of Kitty Gaines and her children. He was a taciturn man who kept to himself and had few close friends. We have no chance to judge the intentions of the elder of the executors who was expected to direct the implementation of John Shumate's will. Unfortunately, he soon followed John Shumate in death. The younger executor he did not know very well, or at least, not well enough.

He signed his will on 21 March 1870. On a cold Friday morning in January, less than three years later John Shumate died, after a lingering illness through which Kitty Gaines was his constant attendant. He was buried on Saturday afternoon on the spot designated in his will, and his careful provisions for marking and protecting that spot were fully met. On Sunday morning his will, all of his papers and books, what money he had on hand and everything else of value, even his gold spectacles, were summarily removed from his house. That was the

James W. Marshall (1822-1910), a native of Clarke Co., Va. Mr. Marshall graduated from Dickinson College, Pa. in 1848 and was for some years a professor at his alma mater. In 1861 President Lincoln appointed him consul at Leeds, England, and in 1869 President U.S. Grant appointed him first assistant postmaster general. Mr. Marshall was living in Paris, Va., when the condition of the heirs of John Shumate was brought to his attention. The Fauquier County Court found the first executor grossly negligent in the management of the estate and appointed Mr. Marshall administrator.

--U. S. Postal Service photo

last Kitty Gaines ever saw of his will, his Bible and Testament or any paper that might have indicated his kind intentions. She could not have read his will if she had seen it, but no one would read it to her.

For Kitty Gaines and her children there followed a decade of utter and abysmal poverty and degradation. The Smith house was never made habitable. The Shumate house was kept locked and empty, stripped even of its furnishings. She and her children were confined to a two-room kitchen building with a loft above, unheated except by the stove. Through the roof the rain poured in buckets. In the loft where Taylor slept, the snow drifted so that, when he arose in the morning, "you could track my son like a rabbit in the snow."[71] There was no schooling. Had there been they could not have gone because they had no shoes. Had they had shoes, they had no books. Once Sarah Catherine pleaded for books. She was told that she already had been given one book, which was enough.

By August of 1884 the condition of Catherine Gaines and her children was so appalling, their testimony as to the treatment they received so distressing, that it attracted the attention of the local judiciary. In the long depositions of neighbors and mere acquaintances made in August of 1884, not one word was said that might be deemed even critical of the wretched family. They were industrious, well behaved and infinitely patient. By their own exertions and immense sacrifice, the girls obtained some education, but not nearly as much as Kitty Gaines wanted for them. Taylor Shumate was a bit of a problem. His angry pride and bitterness led him to injudicious actions. He, according to one deposition, "worked as hard as anyone, white or colored," but his labor got him nowhere. His male pride stung by his inability to care for his womenfolk, his Huguenot blood boiling, he, according to one deposition, and John Webb, his brother-in-law, "stole 40 bushels of wheat out of the granaries on the [Shumate] farm." With the logic of youthful inexperience, he reasoned that he was taking his wheat to feed his starving family.

The court's response to their petition was to dismiss the executor, order the Smith place repaired and made suitable for habitation, and appoint the heirs of Samuel Bayly, owner of *Grafton* as official caretakers of the property and as executors of John Shumate's will. They found the farm in deplorable condition, fences broken down, the woodland ruined by cattle allowed to trample the young trees and the empty house almost ruined. The heirs of Samuel Bayly tried to do what they could but they were themselves in financial difficulty. T. Jackson Bayly, the brother most responsible for the Shumate estate felt oppressed by the problems of the Bayly heirs and frustrated by the slow deliberations of the court. As a consequence, his brothers persuaded him to leave the farm. He was hot-headed, they said, and they feared that he might do something for which he would be sorry later.

During this period the condition of Catherine Gaines and her children improved but slightly. By the end of 1887 the Baylys were insolvent and the work done on the Smith house still unpaid for. It was Sarah Catherine Gaines who found a friend. The children had all been told that if they left the farm they would lose their inheritance. In desperation, she threw caution to the winds and went to Paris, Virginia, to work for James W. Marshall.

James W. Marshall was not of the Fauquier Marshall family unless by some remote and unknown past connection. It is probably better that he was not, as he owed no allegiance to the strangely ambivalent social conscience then prevailing in the county. He was a man of superior education, formerly professor of ancient languages at Dickinson College from which he had been graduated in 1848. During the Lincoln administration he had served as American consul at Leeds, England. President Grant appointed him first assistant postmaster general. In 1887 he was sixty-five and finishing off a distinguished career of public service. He listened to the story of Sarah Catherine Gaines with sympathy and promised to look into it. What he read in the will of John Shumate, on file in the courthouse in Warrenton, shocked him to the core.

True to his promise, he undertook to salvage as much as he could from the wreck of the Shumate estate. On 24 December 1885, on the recommendation of Sarah Catherine Gaines, Adelaide Elizabeth (the wife of John Webb), Taylor Gaines, and Catherine Gaines, Marshall was appointed trustee of the estate under bond of $12,000. Nannie Mason Gaines, still underage, was not mentioned in the instrument. For awhile Marshall tried to manage with the Baylys, but their financial straits were soon apparent. Marshall played his few cards carefully. He was no believer in sympathetic emotion, but he was a believer in the law. After having made the Smith house livable, he insisted that the Gaines family reside there as John Shumate had intended. He found a reputable farmer to rebuild the ruined Shumate farm. For Kitty Gaines and her children, things began to improve.

Meanwhile, Mrs. Marshall helped the Shumate girls get an education of sorts. In 1896 James W. Marshall was seventy-four and felt that the responsibility of trusteeship was too much for him. He recommended Thomas N. Russell as his successor, a change that the Gaines family gladly accepted. By that time Nannie Mason Shumate had married Randolph Dodson. Sarah Catherine Shumate, who was living in Chester, Pennsylvania, had never married. Catherine Gaines died 11 March 1900 and was buried on the Shumate farm. Taylor Scott Shumate died 16 October 1919 and Sarah Catherine Shumate less than a year later, 19 April 1920. Adelaide Elizabeth (Shumate) Webb was also dead before 1927, the year of Nannie Mason (Shumate) Dodson's death. All of the Webb children were also dead. There were seven heirs: Taylor Shumate's four children and three of Nancy Dodson's. They were widely scattered. None of them wanted or could afford to take over the farm where they had suffered such privation. After thirty-two years of quiet trusteeship, Thomas N. Russell sold the place and distributed the proceeds among the heirs.

The purchasers were John T. Ramey and "the Payne boys," youthful sons of Warland M. and Fannie M. (Payne) Payne of Thumb Run.[72] Carroll and Mason Payne worked hard but lost the farm during the depression of the 1930s. The mortgage was purchased by John T. Ramey and the *Payne Place*, along with part of the *Shumate Place* he had purchased, was added to *Grafton*, which he had purchased. The farm was inherited by John M. Ramey from his father and later exchanged with his sister, Eliza Gatewood, for other property.[73]

It is now subdivided into building lots around an artificial lake.

MT. JETT

Alexander Dixon, youngest son of Turner Dixon, sold his inheritance soon after he came of age in 1838. This land was, for the most part, not from the original Turner Dixon grant but had been purchased by Turner Dixon from John Marshall in 1814 [74] and William Rust in 1817.[75] It was east of the Salem-Orlean Grade Road. From it he sold 315.5 acres to Marshall Jett on 29 May 1839.[76]

A considerable effort has been made to connect Marshall Jett to one of the several Jett families living in Fauquier County at the time, but to no avail. Born about 1800, he had been a successful farmer of rented land. He never married and, as far as public records are concerned, was reticent about his personal affairs. He built *Mt. Jett*, which is very much what might be expected of a prosperous bachelor farmer, comfortable, but devoid of architectural pretension.

He was too old to participate in the war, but suffered with the rest the depredation of his livestock and fields. After the war he felt himself too old to manage alone. On 18 June 1870, he deeded *Mount Jett* with 234 acres of his original purchase to George E. DeNeale of Rappahannock County.[77] Along with it went two shares in a tract of 39.75 acres that had belonged to Turner Dixon, but had been overlooked in the division of his estate. In return for this gift it was George DeNeale's duty to provide Marshall Jett with comfortable maintenance during the remainder of his life, plus fifty dollars each year in cash for spending money.

George E. DeNeale was Marshall Jett's nephew. On 21 April 1825, Marshall Jett had signed a security bond for the marriage of Joanna M. Jett, probably his sister, to Daniel Hitt Jr. Two years later, 18 March 1827, Joanna Hitt herself signed a marriage bond for Susanna S. Jett to William S. DeNeale. Then, on 22 September 1828, Daniel Hitt Jr., with Walter Anderson Smith as co-signer, filed a guardian bond for Jane S. Jett, orphan of Birkett Jett. This was done for the sole purpose of enabling Daniel Hitt Jr. to give consent to the marriage of Jane S. Jett, a minor, and M. Mahlon Fulton, which was licensed the same day. If these three women were, as seems likely, sisters of Marshall Jett, then he was the son of Birkett Jett, deceased after 1807 but before 1825.

George E. DeNeale was born 19 April 1830. His father died soon after, and on 6 October 1840 his mother married Thomas M. Drone. George married before 1857, since the first child of whom we have record was born in 1858. His wife was named Martha, and though we have no specific record of her family name, she was almost certainly Martha E. Grant, daughter of Turner D. and Elizabeth F. (Nelson) Grant. The marriage record of Turner D. Grant and Elizabeth F. Nelson, daughter of Thomas Nelson, is recorded in Fauquier County, 22 December 1828. Their daughter, Martha E., was born 17 April 1837. Elizabeth, wife of T. D. Grant, died at *Mount Jett* at the age of eighty-three years.

The children of George E. and Martha (Grant) De Neale are known from headstones in the DeNeale family burying ground at *Mount Jett* and from family records.[78] There was Lizzie E. DeNeale, born 7 April 1858, who died unmarried at the age of twenty-three. Next came W. D. DeNeale--born 23 August 1861. He died at the age of thirty, also probably unmarried. There were five more girls: May, Ida (both May and Ida married Frank M. Walter), Lena (who married George Shannon and had two children: Maurice, who died young, and Martha, who married St. George Raby), Nannie (who married Jeffrey

Mt. Jett. Left portion of log construction, possibly built by Marshall Jett, who purchased 315.5 acres from Alexander Dixon in 1839. Right section built by George E. DeNeale who bought the property from Marshall Jett in 1870. --photo by author

St. Andrews Episcopal Church

St. Andrews-on-the-Hill is located on Rt. 647 at Ada. The congregation traces its beginning to a community Sunday School founded by Mr. Shirley Latham and Rev. Wilfred E. Roach in a nearby schoolhouse. The first teachers were Mrs. J. Stevens Mason and her daughter, Eliza Green, of Emmanuel Episcopal Church near Delaplane. In 1919, the trustees of Piedmont Parish purchased property across the road and began construction of a Blue Ridge Mission Chapel. It was built by Mr. John E. Russell of Orlean in 1922. The Rev. W. B. Everett became rector in 1921, serving the church until 1941. During this time, the congregation grew and a mission home nearby was acquired. The church is located within Leeds Parish.

--courtesy of John T. Toler of *The Fauquier Times-Democrat*

Ada School, ca. 1927. This school was located on the road between Moreland and Ada, now Route 724. In the early 1930s the pupils were bused to Marshall and the Ada School was dismantled and moved to Marshall to become an annex to the Marshall High School.

--courtesy of the late Raymond H. Lee

Buchanan and had no children), and Mattie (who married Herbert Grant and had a son, DeNeale Grant).

There was also Nelson J. DeNeale, who was born in 1866 and died 1950 and married Ada Gay Payne (1877-1958), daughter of Richard Cumberland and Melissa Almira (McKennie) Payne. It was for Ada (Payne) DeNeale that the nearby village of Ada was named.[79]

The date of Marshall Jett's death is unknown. George DeNeale placed a handsome marble headstone at his grave, which is about as uninformative as a grave marker can be. It gives only his name. As George DeNeale was rather liberal with information on the headstones marking the graves of the rest of his family, his reticence in this instance is probably attributable to the wishes of the old man himself. He allowed no one to invade his privacy, even in death.

On 1 January 1883, George DeNeale began picking up additional shares in the 39.75 acre tract adjacent to his property, which was useless to the Dixon heirs.[80] The heirs were scattered and it took him until November 1897 to obtain clear title with the help of Robert Scott, one of the heirs.[81] He also bought, 21 December 1883, about 27 acres known as the "Marshall Jett tract" which had been conveyed by James Rogers to Benjamin F. Rixey in 1855.[82]

George DeNeale died on 16 February 1912. His wife survived him almost exactly five years. Their deceased daughter's husband, F. M. Walter, later took possession of *Mount Jett* as a result of a chancery suit, the details of which are somewhat obscure. His second wife (sister of his first wife, Ida) conveyed it, 31 July 1919,[83] to Thomas E. Lunceford, who, in 1928, willed it to his son, William L. Lunceford.[84] Mason F. Lunceford, son of William L. and Mary E. Lunceford, was deeded 285.5 acres on 2 May 1974, by his parents. Mr. Lunceford still farms the hilly acres of *Mount Jett* and cherishes the Jett-DeNeale-Lunceford homestead as much as his predecessors.

CLEVELAND or PIEDMONT FARM

Andrew Barbee, who purchased Edward Dixon's 254-acre share of the original division of the Turner Dixon grant, 31 October 1833, from the feckless young heir, was in his forties at the time.[85] Young Dixon, having taken to the bottle rather enthusiastically, was overanxious to get rid of the farm. Later, he complained that his brother, George B. Dixon, should not have allowed him to do so "knowing his weakness." As a matter of fact, for Andrew Barbee, too, the sale was a mistake.

Born about 1790, Andrew Barbee had married Louisa Smith, daughter of Captain Joseph Smith of *Hickoryville*, sixteen years before. They lived in Salem, where Barbee was, to all outward appearances, a successful merchant.[86] In 1824 he bought Lot 31 in Salem from his wife's uncle, John Puller Smith. Smith had built a house on the lot, in which Andrew Barbee and his wife lived and operated as an ordinary. His wife, though, was not too keen on the life of an innkeeper's wife, and longed for a home not subject to the importunities of paying guests.

Captain Joseph Smith's estate was substantial and Andrew Barbee confidently expected that his wife's inheritance would be sufficient to finance the investment. Though outwardly prosperous, his financial condition was in a somewhat precarious state. Captain Smith must have sensed this, and when Smith died, Barbee discovered to his utter dismay that Captain Smith's will effectively placed his daughter's inheritance well beyond her husband's reach. Already over-extended, Barbee was forced, within less than a year of his purchase of the Dixon property, to mortgage it to secure a debt to John Withers of Alexandria.

There had been on the property when Barbee bought it an old, one-storey frame tenant house shown on the survey of the original Turner Dixon grant in 1821. There was also a stone spring house on the line that divided his land from that of George B. Dixon. No trace of either structure remains today and they were probably in a dilapidated condition even then. Hoping for a turn for the better, Barbee went ahead with his plans for a "new dwelling house, outhouses, barns, stables, shops, orchards, etc.," mentioned in the deed of 1837.[87] In addition he bought 96 acres of the Turner Dixon, Jr. dividend of the original grant from George Beverley Dixon when the latter moved to Mississippi in 1835.

By 28 March 1837, Andrew Barbee's affairs had deteriorated even further. He was then forced to obtain a second mortgage to secure his indebtedness to William Foote, a wealthy landowner in Prince William County. Five years later, 30 December 1842, he placed the entire property, then about 355 acres, as well as two improved lots in Salem and one vacant lot, in trust to secure his many debts including the two mentioned above. He stated without apology that his inability to use his wife's money had forced him into this awkward position. On 4 September 1844, the game was up. The property was sold at public auction. Andrew Barbee and Louisa, his wife, joined in giving clear title to Hugh Rogers, Jr., the highest bidder.[88]

Hugh Rogers, Jr. was a brother of James Rogers who had bought *Vermont* from Henry Dixon in 1836. He and his wife, Mary, (nee Mary Hawling, sister of the wife of Hugh's brother James) owned the property only eight years. While he was there he sold 7.5 acres of land to Samuel Bayly in 1849 [89] and bought an additional 50 acres on the Little Cobbler Mountain from Turner Adams.[90] He also entered into a verbal agreement with the sponsors of a schoolhouse to be built on his property, assuring them rights of access and tenure. However, the Rogers were not living on the property on 17 February 1852, when they sold it to his kinsman, Gibson Gregg.[91]

The next owner, Gibson Gregg, was allied to the Rogers family by marriage. He was living at *Cleveland* when the deed was signed. It is not known when the old Barbee Place was first called *Cleveland* but it appears that the name was given it by Gregg during his brief tenure. Hugh Rogers sold the property under the condition that his obligations to the sponsors of the schoolhouse be continued by his successor. However, Gibson Gregg owned *Cleveland* less than three years. He was, apparently, a large landowner in Fauquier and Loudoun Counties. In 1865 he was among those prominent ex-Confederates who were notified that their lands would be confiscated for distribution among the Freedmen.[92] The order was later rescinded, but *Cleveland* having been previously sold, was not threatened.

William R. Jones, who bought *Cleveland* from Gibson Gregg, 29 December 1854, was a man of considerable means.[93] Furthermore, he was married to Alice P. Rixey, sister of Benjamin F. Rixey of *Vermont*, who had been given a large estate by her father. They lived there with their two small children until his death in 1859. In his will, dated 14 February 1859, Jones named his brother, John T. Jones, executor, giving him a free hand to invest his estate, most of which was in securities and slaves, for the benefit of his children. John T. Jones did not foresee the day, soon to come, when the slaves would be freed and the securities worthless. He bought the western half of *Eastwood* as an investment and other land.[94]

John T. Jones apparently realized that the unsuccessful outcome of the war would be ruinous for his brother's estate as early as December of 1862. At that time he and Captain Samuel Rixey, acting for his grandchildren, entered into a contract with Decatur Bainbridge Hall of Warren County to purchase *Cleveland* for $20,000. This agreement was not recorded until 7 December 1866, when the war was over.[95] It was all really a family affair. Decatur B. Hall (1815-1871) was the husband of Louisa Herndon Love Rixey, daughter of Richard Rixey III and his second wife, Penelope Gibbs. She was Alice P. (Rixey) Jones's first cousin. Hall owned a great amount of land in Warren County and certainly did not disturb the widow and her two children at *Cleveland* as long as the war lasted. They had troubles enough.[96]

It is not certain that Decatur B. Hall and his wife ever occupied *Cleveland*. In the subsequent years Alice (Rixey) Jones died, and, presumably, her children went their separate ways. Hall was, for some years before his death, a merchant in Salem, and at that time he may have lived there. He died, however, on 17 August 1871, at his home near Front Royal and was buried there. He did, during his tenure, add 122 acres to the *Cleveland* property, across the Salem-Hume road, (the old Dixon's Quarter Road). At the time of his death it contained 522 acres. There was a considerable amount of litigation over his estate and his heirs were unable to dispose of *Cleveland* until 31 July 1882.[97]

The purchaser was Robert Avenel Beverley (1861-1904) son of William and Frances Westwood (Gray) Beverley of *Selma*, Loudoun County.[98] He married, in 1881, Julia Duval of *Prospect Hill* near Frederick, Maryland.[99] The Beverleys lived at *Grafton* and, apparently, leased out *Cleveland* to others during their ownership. Robert A. Beverley died in 1904. On 11 April 1906, L. Kemp Duval, executor and trustee of the estate of Robert A. Beverley, sold the property to Frederick W. Okie and Sydney Paget of New York. The price was $20,975, an increase of less than $1,000 over its previous sale in 1862.[100] Paget, an Englishman, was a partner in the deal, but does not appear to have figured further in the history of *Cleveland*. Frederick W. and Pauline (Platt) Okie greatly improved the property which was showing signs of neglect after years of absentee ownership. They renamed it *Piedmont Farm*, an appropriate name. If ever a place could be said to lie "at the foot of the mountain," this one answers that description.

VERNON MILLS

One of the smallest but certainly most interesting parcels of land carved from the original Turner Dixon tract is certainly *Vernon Mills*. Its history begins in 1814. On 31 May of that year, Turner Dixon bought 102 acres on Thumb Run from John Marshall.[101] There he built a grist mill which is shown on Charles Kemper's plat of Leeds Manor dated 2 July 1815.

When the first division of the estate of Turner Dixon was made in 1821, this land, with an additional 178 acres from the original grant, fell to the lot of his son, William Dixon, then ten years old. This young man died before reaching his twenty-first birthday.[102] His land was sold by his brother, George B. Dixon, on 2 November 1832.[103] Most of it, more than 248 acres, he sold to Maria Willis. Miss Willis, a spinster, was born in Gloucester County 23 September 1784. She was probably a descendant of Colonel Henry Willis, a large landowner in that county, and was the aunt of Claudia H. Burwell, wife of James Keith Marshall of *Moreland* and *Leeds*. Maria Willis probably never lived on the land, as she died three years later, 5 October 1835, at the age of forty-nine. Her executor, James Keith Marshall, a son of John Marshall, put up her land for auction. It was bought in by Edward Carrington Marshall, his brother.[104] It thus became part of the Marshall estate which continued in that family for generations. Maria Willis's land was never part of *Vernon Mills*.

The remainder of William Dixon's land, amounting to a little more than 34 acres, with the mill, was sold on the same day to Captain James Morehead for $594. It was this land that was to form the nucleus of *Vernon Mills*.[105]

Adjoining this property at the extreme south end of the Turner Dixon grant, there is shown on Kemper's map of 1815 a tract of land containing 673 acres belonging to Captain Joseph Smith. Captain Smith, born about 1750, may be the same Joseph Smith who was commissioned as a lieutenant in the Fauquier Militia in 1781 by the Fauquier County Court. With two names seen as often in combination as Joseph and Smith, it is difficult to be certain. There were several Smith families in Fauquier County at the time.

Captain Joseph Smith was also very probably a brother of John Winn Smith (1745-1811) of Fredericksburg. Identical family names were carried down in both families and there were several intermarriages among their descendants. On Kemper's plat of Leeds Manor, dated 1815, there is also shown a large tract of land around Orlean belonging to John Puller Smith, eldest son of John Winn Smith and nephew of Captain Joseph Smith.

Captain Joseph Smith and his wife, whose family name is unknown, had at least two sons and four daughters. Two daughters married into the Adams family, one married Andrew Barbee and one married her cousin, James Whitacre Smith. On Captain Joseph Smith's death his sons shared his estate, one of whom was Willis Golder Smith, 1777-1820. Willis Golder Smith married 10 February 1805 his first cousin, Sarah (Sally)

Smith, daughter of John Winn and Margaret (Puller) Smith.

In 1811 John Winn Smith died, leaving his daughter Sally Smith a substantial estate, mostly in Negroes. Her estate was left in trust with his son, John Puller Smith, "for the sole use and benefit of my beloved daughter Sally and her heirs forever, and to no other intent whatever." John Winn Smith had quarreled with one of his sons-in-law, Thomas Hughes, and as a result of the experience, placed little confidence in the others. Everything left to his three daughters was placed in trust.

Willis Golder Smith died in 1820, leaving seven children, four sons and three daughters. The youngest son, Willis Golder, Jr., died at the age of thirteen, but the three oldest, James Golder, Joseph B., and John Puller Smith, survived. Of the three daughters, Margaret P. Smith married James T. Ball and moved to Missouri; Mary married a cousin, John Thomas Smith and moved to Harrison County, Virginia; and the youngest, Sally Ann Lucy Smith, married George W. Davis, who figures later in our story.[107]

When Captain James Morehead bought what later became *Vernon Mills* from the William Dixon estate, Sally (Smith) Smith was living with her sons, Joseph, aged twenty-two, and John P. Smith, aged nineteen, on the property adjoining Morehead's purchase. Its advantages did not then appeal to her, or she would have bought it herself.

The old Dixon grist mill on the property did not fill Captain Morehead's needs. Instead of attempting to bring the old mill up to date, he elected to move downstream and build an entirely new merchant mill along modern lines. He apparently left the old mill in operation, since the name applied to them later, *Vernon Mills*, is always found in the plural. The new mill operated until 1938. In its later years it was run by a steam engine except for two days a week when water-ground meal was ground. There was not enough water in Thumb Run by that time to do more.

Captain James Morehead died in January of 1847. In the division of his estate the ownership of the mills became a complicated issue. In the appraisal of the estate, the "upper mill" (or Dixon's old mill) was valued at $400. The new "lower mill" was valued at $2,000. His daughter, Eleanora Morehead, then married to Benjamin F. Rixey, was awarded the upper mill and one-half the lower mill. The other one-half of the lower mill was awarded to her brother, James Milton Morehead. Such divided ownership of the mills had obvious drawbacks.[108]

The mills were therefore put up for sale, and this time Sally (Smith) Smith, widow, did not miss her opportunity to

Vernon Mills, home of George B. Davis, inherited from his father, George W. Davis. Built by Willis Golder Smith between 1847 and 1857. --photo by author

George W. Davis, merchant and owner of *Vernon Mills*.

--courtesy of the late James Davis

secure a fine, income-producing property for her sons. A large house was built on the property between 1847 and 1857. All of this was financed in large measure by the sale of slaves, children of the Negroes left her by her father.

Sally Smith died 24 November 1857. A suit was brought in chancery in January 1858 over the division of her estate, which was large. By that time, John Puller Smith, her brother and trustee of her estate, had been dead twenty years. Replacing him as trustees were her second and third sons, Joseph B. and John Puller Smith, the younger. The suit was brought by her eldest son, James Golder Smith, for an accounting of the sale of Negroes from the estate during the preceding ten years, in large measure to purchase real estate. James G. Smith wanted to be certain that he and his sisters got their proper share.

The other sons responded that the slaves had been sold under their authority as trustees, at their mother's express direction. They also argued that they had been a great care and responsibility and that, in fact, it had been necessary to sell some to satisfy the claims on their grandfather's estate by Thomas Hughes, the son-in-law with whom John Winn Smith had been at loggerheads when he wrote his will over fifty years before.[109]

Without going into the details of the chancery suit, which is long and complicated, it is sufficient to say that the court had little alternative to ordering the sale of the *Vernon Mills* property to satisfy the contesting claimants. It is at this time that the name "Vernon Mills" is first used in public records. Why or by whom this name was chosen remains a mystery. It was supposed to contain "about 140 acres" in addition to the mills.

Fortunately one of the heirs, George W. Davis, husband of Sally Ann Lucy Smith, was willing to buy out the other heirs. When the property was offered for sale at auction on 27 December 1859, he was the highest bidder at thirty dollars per acre. A survey was made by George W. Norris on 28 March 1860. The tract of land from the old property of Captain Joseph Smith, across the road to the east of the Turner Dixon grant was found to contain a little more than 96 acres. The *Vernon Mills* site, including the dwelling, was surveyed at 41 acres.[110]

Protest came immediately, probably from Edward Carrington Marshall, who was still living. How in the world, he asked, had the mill tract sold by George B. Dixon to James Morehead in 1832 as something over 34 acres, become 41 acres in 1860? George W. Norris was asked to take another look at the record. On 12 April 1860, he was bound to admit that he had no good answer. George W. Davis was short some seven acres of land he believed he had bought, necessitating an adjustment in the purchase price.

The house at *Vernon Mills* stands today, high above the now ruined mill, a spacious, well-built structure, with simple detail. It descended by agreement between four sons of George W. Davis, to George Beauregard Davis, named for his father's old commander in 1862.[111] George B. Davis married Medora Stephenson, but they had no children. During his tenure at *Vernon Mills*, George B. Davis operated a small store in the yard. There was a post office there from 1873 to 1920. After his death in 1943, *Vernon Mills* reverted to his last surviving brother, Willis Golder Davis, according to the terms explicit in his father's will. Willis Golder Davis deeded the property to his daughter, Golda (Davis) Pollock, wife of Dr. Joseph Pollock.[112]

MORELAND

The land called *Moreland* lies west of the Turner Dixon grant on the northeast slope of the Big Cobbler Mountain. Its original boundaries are unknown, but it was within the immense area purchased by John Marshall, James Markham Marshall, and Raleigh Colston from the Fairfax heirs in 1806. Apparently it fell within the territory allotted to Chief Justice John Marshall, as, in 1833, it was owned by his son, James Keith Marshall.[113] In 1821 James Keith Marshall had married Claudia Hamilton Burwell, daughter of Nathaniel Burwell, and settled at *Moreland*, where their four oldest children were born.[114] Nothing is known to remain of the house in which they lived. After the birth of their fourth child, Maria Willis Marshall, on 31 March 1828, they moved to *Leeds*, another Marshall estate near Hume.[115]

Before March 1833, the Marshalls deeded about 200 acres of *Moreland* to a member of the Turner family of Fauquier County. This family was not, apparently, related to the Turner family previously associated with the Dixon Valley, but were descended from Captain Hezekiah Turner, a Revolutionary War officer prominent in Fauquier history during that period. This land was on both sides of the road to Markham about one-half mile west of its junction with the road from Salem to Hume, or, Dixon's Quarter Road.

On 15 March 1833, only a month after the Dixon dower division had been authorized, James Keith Marshall and Claudia, his wife, conveyed a large part of the tract known as *Moreland* to Turner Adams for $4,050.[116] This land, a little more than 713 acres between the Big and Little Cobbler Mountains, adjoined the Dixon grant on the west, extending a considerable distance along the Salem-Hume Road and was on both sides of the road to Markham. It touched the Turner tract on three sides.

Turner Adams was related by marriage to the Marshall family. He was a son of George and Ann (Turner) Adams, his mother having been another descendant of Captain Hezekiah Turner. He married his first cousin, Mary ("Mollie") Smith, daughter of Thomas and Elizabeth (Adams) Smith. Her grandmother was Elizabeth (Marshall) Smith, a sister of Colonel Thomas Marshall, father of the Chief Justice. In a sense, Turner Adams's purchase of the *Moreland* property was all in the family.[117]

Turner and Mary (Smith) Adams had seven children, two boys and five girls. The eldest, Anna D. Adams, married, in 1841, her cousin, John Smith. Then followed Mary Elizabeth

Smith Adams, who married John W. Newman; Martha Turner Adams, who married William F. Turner; George Turner Adams, who married a first cousin, Jane L. Adams; Lucy Jane Adams, who married George Louthan Kerfoot of Clarke County; John A. Adams; and Agnes Eliza Adams, who married James T. Turner. James T. Turner was heir to the Turner tract adjoining.

Turner Adams and his wife lived at *Moreland*, presumably in the house that had been occupied by the Marshalls. However, he owned other property, sufficient to provide estates for his two sons and younger daughters. After his wife's death he had no interest in holding the property together in a single tract which, because of its peculiar shape, was difficult to manage. Its position in a narrow valley between two hills meant also that much of it was steep and heavily wooded.

In September 1842 Turner Adams, for "$1 and natural love and affection," deeded 136 acres to his daughter, Mary E. S. Newman.[118] This part of the tract was across the Salem-Hume Road from the land Andrew Barbee had bought from Edward Dixon in 1833. The Newmans owned this beautiful property only four years. On 6 October 1846, they sold it, then known as *Glenwood*, to Captain Lewis Tracy.[119] On the death of Captain Tracy in 1860, *Glenwood* was sold by the trustee of his estate, James Vass Brooke, to Thomas Glascock.[120]

The next partition of *Moreland* came three years later when, on 4 December 1845, Turner Adams conveyed to John Smith and George L. Kerfoot of Clarke County, "for the love and affection the said Turner Adams bears his said sons-in-law, Smith and Kerfoot and their wives Annie, wife of John Smith, and Lucy, wife of George L. Kerfoot," 200.5 acres, part of the land on which he had formerly lived, which he had bought of James Keith Marshall.[121] This 200.5 acres was also along the Salem-Hume Road opposite the land, later called *Silver Spring*, bought by Dr. Thomas T. Withers in 1844 from the heirs of John Dixon. Neither of the beneficiaries of this gift seems to have been interested in moving on to the property.

Instead, we find a complicated deed, dated 11 October 1847, between George L. and Lucy (Adams) Kerfoot and John and Ann (Adams) Smith, of the first part; James T. Turner of the second part; and Martha T. Turner, wife of William F. Turner, of the third part, in which the land deeded to Kerfoot and Smith is sold to James T. Turner for $2,250.[122] It is specifically related in the deed that the land was across the road from *Vermont* at the base of the Big Cobbler Mountain and adjoined a small tract recently surveyed for Dr. John W. Newman (possibly for his office). From it was deducted 8 acres which were deeded directly to James T. Turner. The rest was to be held by him "for the sole use and behoof of Martha T. Turner, wife of William F. Turner."

Some aspects of this deed are not explained. Martha Turner, wife of William F. Turner, had been Martha T. Adams, daughter of Turner Adams. It is not specifically stated whether William F. Turner was dead or otherwise incapacitated. James T. Turner may have been a brother of William F. Turner. He was certainly at that time the owner of the Turner tract that adjoined the 200 acres on the west. He had married Agnes Eliza Adams, youngest daughter of Turner Adams, as previously stated.

On the small property deeded him, James T. Turner built a store southwest of the road to Markham (Rte. 724). Here, between 1 July 1848 and 30 June 1849, James T. Turner, postmaster, sold $12.45 worth of stamps for which he got $10.65 in compensation. Even then the post office had a slim margin of profit.

On the day after Christmas 1849, possibly as a present on that occasion, John Smith and Ann D., his wife, together with George L. Kerfoot and Lucy J., his wife, deeded one-half acre adjoining the store to Hezekiah Turner as trustee of the four infant daughters of James T. and Agnes (Adams) Turner.[123] The need for this trusteeship is also unknown. James T. Turner lived until he was sixty-five in 1882 and his wife survived him by three years.

On 23 February 1846 Turner Adams made the last major sale from the tract purchased from James Keith Marshall in 1833. He sold 295.25 acres to George Washington Shacklett. This land was on both sides of the Markham Road, west of the Turner tract. The road separated it almost entirely from the rest of Turner Adams's land. The only connection was a small tract of 50 acres of woodland on the slope of the Little Cobbler. Somewhere on the property George W. Shacklett and his brother apparently operated a tavern. However, Shacklett sold the property before his death to Benjamin Harrison. In December 1868 his widow, Lucinda (Smith) Shacklett, and his children, M. Bettie Shacklett and Turner D. Shacklett, confirmed the sale after Harrison had sold the eastern two-thirds of the land to William Pearson and the remainder to Joseph Ballard.[124]

Turner Adams sold the 50-acre tract on the side of the Little Cobbler, 28 February 1851, to Hugh Rogers, Jr. Rogers had bought *Cleveland* six years before and this land was presumably valuable for the timber on it as, by then, most of the woodland in the valley had been cleared. With this last

Clarendon. Purchased in 1851 by B. F. Rixey from heirs of John Marshall, Jr., who had inherited this portion of the Manor of Leeds called *The Pines* from his father, Chief Justice John Marshall. In 1861 Mr. Rixey sold the 292-acre tract to Robert Scott who kept a few acres and sold 271 acres to Ludwell Lake, Sr. in 1869. Ludwell Lake, Jr. obtained the farm from his father in 1871. The house was built during the Lakes' ownership. In 1884 Mr. Lake sold the farm to his nephew, Charles Rixey Lake, who failed to make payments due on purchase debts dating back to the Marshall ownership. The farm was sold under decree of the court in 1896 to L. E. Woodward who lived on the property until his death in 1956. --author photo recorded sale all but 32 acres of Turner Adams's purchase from James Keith Marshall are accounted for. There is no further record of Turner Adams in the deed books, and the date of his death is unknown.

By 1855 James T. Turner was apparently willing to abandon his role as proprietor of a crossroads country store. The store itself had been built on the half acre that belonged to his children. As trustee, Hezekiah Turner sold it 18 September 1855,[125] and on 6 October, James T. Turner, as trustee for Martha T. Turner, wife of William F. Turner, sold 2.5 acres adjacent to it from her estate.[126] The purchaser was Rachael A. Hitch, whose history is another curious chapter in the story of the Dixon Valley.

In April of 1785, Judith Marshall, the beautiful and vivacious daughter of Colonel Thomas and Mary Randolph (Keith) Marshall, married very much against her parents' wishes George Brooke, son of Humphrey and Ann (Whiting) Brooke of Fauquier County.[127] There was certainly no objection to the Brooke family, which was one of considerable distinction. The objection arose because of the extreme youth of the young couple and the fact that George Brooke, despite a "prepossessing person and fascinating manners" had already acquired a reputation for dissipation, idleness and profligacy.[128]

Nevertheless, the marriage took place and the young couple moved to Lewis County, Kentucky, where they maintained little contact with the rest of the family. They had seven children, among them George Brooke, Jr., the only one of the four sons to marry. His wife was named Rachael, and there is some indication that she came from Fauquier County, but her family name remains a mystery. The younger George Brooke died before 1846, leaving five children. His widow married John Hitch in Fauquier County (bond dated 21 February 1846). In the bond her name is given as Rachael Ann Brooke, widow; James Revell was bondsman and Daniel James Payne of *Chestnut Lawn* was a witness. Payne was then Deputy Clerk of the Fauquier County Court.

The reason that Rachael Hitch wanted this tiny fragment of the once vast Marshall estate is a matter for conjecture. On 17 April 1869, she deeded it to her son, Robert H. Brooke, for natural love and affection--and $200.[129] He died three years later, leaving it back to her for life, after which one-half was to go to his sister Mary, then married to George B. Bradford, and one-fourth each to his brothers John and Frank Brooke. On the death of Rachael Hitch before December 1873, there seemed to be no one to represent the estate. Because there were liens against the shares of John and Frank Brooke, the court ordered the property sold at auction. Mary (Brooke) Bradford bought it in, with the help of Benjamin F. Rixey.[130] When Rixey himself fell into financial difficulty, he was obliged to demand payment of the loan.[131] However, Mrs. Bradford was able to arrange postponement until she was able to sell it to John H. Lee in 1883.[132]

The properties in the Turner Dixon grant with which we are concerned were not part of the original *Moreland* but, through later association and common ownership, have long been considered so. The first of these involved the land sold by Charles C. Dixon in 1836 to George Adams.[133] Charles C. Dixon's share of his father's estate was in four parcels, 254 acres from the first division, 66 acres of woodland, 17 acres adjoining James Morehead and 51.5 acres of cleared land some distance away. The last three were from the division of his mother's dower lands. George Adams bought the first three of these tracts, totaling 337 acres. He almost immediately sold the 17-acre tract to James Morehead, 5 February 1838, leaving himself with 320 acres.[134]

George Adams was a son of George and Ann (Turner) Adams and, presumably, a brother of Turner Adams. The subsequent history of his family is both complicated and obscure. After his death his land was divided among his heirs and much of it passed out of the family. Before the end of the century there remained only 107.5 acres known as the *Ned Adams Place*. Presumably it belonged to an Edward Adams, son or grandson of George Adams, who sold it before 1901 to John H. Lee.[135]

In 1867 a third George Adams arrived upon the scene, according to the record in Fauquier County. He was a son of Littleton Adams, a brother of the first George Adams who married Ann Turner. He was, therefore, a first cousin of George Adams mentioned above and of Turner Adams. In some way he had acquired the property set aside in 1847 for the "use and behoof" of Martha (Adams) Turner. To this property of 108 acres he had added a nearly square tract of 35 acres to the south that had not been part of Turner Adams's purchase from James Keith Marshall. George Adams, 1786-1868, had lived on the property at least since 1859.

There is an old cemetery on the property in a locust grove, long neglected and overgrown. In it are buried George Adams, Ann R. Adams, his wife (1801-1879), four daughters and one son, all of whom, except Ann R. Adams, died before 1868. All of the children were between eighteen and thirty-four years of age. Therefore, when George Adams and Ann R., his

Store built by Henry Lake Lee on land formerly owned by George Adams. The Adams cemetery is located on a knoll to the right and behind the store. This was also one of the last barrooms in Fauquier County. --photo by author

John H. Lee and wife standing outside their lawn fence at *Moreland*.

—courtesy of the late Raymond H. Lee

wife, sold this property to Thomas Glascock 30 September 1867, they were both very old and had lost five children in the preceding eight years.[136] The son, George L. Adams, twenty-six at the time of his death, may have been killed in the war.

Thomas Glascock, 1814-1885, was a son of Aquilla Glascock of *Rockburn*, Fauquier County. He had gone to Missouri during the war but had returned to Virginia after the death of his first wife. He was one of the largest landowners in Fauquier at the time of his death. Having bought the Lewis Tracy land *Glenwood* in 1860,[137] he owned 284 acres of *Moreland*, which he called his Cobbler Mountain Farm.[138] He never lived there. He had four sons but only one survived him, Bedford Glascock, 1850-1929, who inherited the property.[139]

On both sides of the Glascock *Cobbler Mountain Farm*, John H. Lee was acquiring land before the turn of the century. He bought the *Kerfoot Place* (49.5 acres) and the Turner tract (182 acres) from the heirs of William F. and Martha (Adams) Turner and the heirs of James T. Turner. It appears from a deed dated 18 October 1887 that Martha (Adams) Turner had sold the *Kerfoot Place* to James T. Turner during her lifetime, but had never given him a deed. The latter, in turn, sold it to William H. Kerfoot, with similar negligence.[140] In 1887 the matter was straightened out, and, in 1894, John H. Lee bought both parcels, totaling 231.5 acres.[141] In addition he bought 48 acres of dense woodland on the side of the Big Cobbler Mountain from the Marshalls.

Lee also bought the Moreland store and the three acres adjacent to it. The Lees did not live in either the Kerfoot or Turner houses, but, instead, made their home in the dwelling house on the three acres next to the store. From the Turner Dixon grant on the east side of the Marshall-Hume Road he bought the *Ned Adams Place*, (107.5 acres) mentioned earlier, and 89 acres from the Jones tract called *Silver Spring*.[142] Of this, 36 acres came from Robert A. Beverley of *Cleveland*, and the remainder from Jones himself. Beverley also sold him 8 acres of *Cleveland*, so that his deed from him is for 44 acres.

When John H. Lee died in 1901 he left an estate of 486 acres in scattered locations to be divided between his second wife and the three children of his first wife, or their heirs.[143] One of these, Carroll A. Lee, was dead, leaving three children. Elizabeth A. Lee, the only daughter, was married to Alpheus Weaver. Henry Lake Lee, the surviving son, was administrator of his father's estate. In the division of the estate the children of Carroll A. Lee were given the Turner house and 152 acres south of the Markham Road. Elizabeth Weaver was given the *Kerfoot Place* and 44 acres from the Turner tract and the woodland above it, bought from the Marshalls, plus the 53-acre tract from *Silver Spring*. In 1906 the Weavers sold the *Kerfoot Place* to Edward Ramey.[144] They had already sold the *Silver Spring* tract to her brother, Henry L. Lee.

Mary Lee, the second wife of John H. Lee, was a daughter of William Pearson who had bought two-thirds of the Shacklett Farm. As part of her dower, she was given 37 acres that her husband had bought from James T. Turner's heirs, adjoining her father's farm. She retained possession of her home at the Moreland store. Finally, she was awarded the 44 acres acquired from Robert Beverley. In 1932, the heirs of John H. Lee sold the dower land to William A. Fishback.[145]

Henry Lake Lee took the *Ned Adams Place* as a nucleus around which he would build one of the finest estates in Fauquier County. He was an ambitious man and that, at least, was his goal. The first order of business was to obtain as much as possible of the land once owned by George Adams. About 54 acres at the south end had been irretrievably lost to *Vermont*, later *Glenara*. He bought the remaining 93 acres, giving him 200 acres of the Charles C. Dixon dividend. He expanded this eastward to include much of Alice (Dixon) Payne's share of the original Turner Dixon grant. This, with the 54 acres bought from his sister, gave him 400 acres east of the Marshall-Hume Road.

On the west side of that road Henry L. Lee bought two properties. In 1913 Bedford Glascock sold the land his father had bought from George Adams to F. M. Walter.[146] Walter held it five years and sold it to Browning Payne.[147] Payne divided it into three lots, the northernmost of which, 33 acres next to the Moreland store, he sold to Edward Ramey who owned the *Kerfoot Place* adjoining.[148] The remaining land he sold in 1922 to Henry L. Lee, together with an adjacent triangle high on the Big Cobbler Mountain. Lee also bought a strange piece of land less than 500 feet wide but nearly two-thirds of a mile long, starting at the Marshall-Hume Road and making a beeline from the top of the Big Cobbler. Mr. Lee wanted this for the spring, which he had piped to his home.

In 1905 Henry Lee replaced the old farmhouse with a large, comfortable house on or near the site of the old Adams home. He also maintained a barroom in a small building about halfway between his house and the Moreland store. Old timers' stories of "wild times" spent at *Moreland* probably emanated from Lee's Barroom. The Volstead Act, of course, ended its days.

After forty-three years of intensive and very successful farming, in 1927, Henry Lake Lee decided that he had earned a rest. His farm was offered for sale. Although his father's holdings had, collectively, been known as *Moreland*, the only part to which that name was attached was the three acres known as *Old Moreland*, which he did not own. Similarly, nowhere in the elaborate 17-page brochure of the Henry Lee Estate, prepared before its sale, is the place referred to as "Moreland."

The brochure pauses for a moment in time to describe the land, with its herd of prize-winning cattle, its dairy cows and its rolling fields of corn and wheat. The house was a "city house" with "Delco electric lights, running water piped from a mountain spring, bathroom, telephone, etc." Not many houses in Fauquier had such amenities more than fifty years ago. The sale was advertised to take place on 18 July 1927. As an inducement to attend, with no strings attached, a new Ford Touring Car and unspecified "Gifts of Gold" were given away. The gold, no doubt, came from Mr. Lee's pocket. The Ford Touring Car is a reminder that, among his other interests, Henry Lake Lee was the founder of "Ford Authorized Sales," the first automobile sales and service establishment in Marshall. Although Lee had sold this business in 1926, he doubtless had maintained connections who could arrange for him to obtain cars at a substantial discount.[149]

The property, except for 122 acres across the road, was bought by Leonidas Lake Triplett, whose wife had inherited the *White House*. The deed from Henry L. Lee and Estelle P. Lee, his wife, is dated 18 October 1927.[150] The remaining 122 acres west of the Marshall-Hume Road was the land Lee had bought from Browning Payne in 1922. It was bought by W. E. Matthews, who had bought the *Kerfoot Place* from the heirs of Edward L. Ramey in 1927.[151] Matthews combined parts of both purchases into a single tract of 108 acres, having most of the same boundaries as that sold by George Adams to Thomas Glascock in 1867. If any property has the right to be called *Moreland*, this one does, as on it stood the original house occupied by the Marshalls a hundred and fifty years ago. Matthews sold it in 1928 to Robert Cary Ashby, whose daughter married Julian Winter Rector.[152] As Mr. Rector also owns *Glenwood*, nearly half of Turner Adams's original 713 acres is back under a single ownership.

Notes for Chapter 3

1. Aurelia M. Jewell, Loudoun County, *Virginia Marriage Bonds, 1762-1850*, (Berryville: Chesapeake Book Co., c11962), p. 31. License was issued to James Rogers and Martha Hawling, ward of Hamilton Rogers, 20 Nov. 1830.
2. Fauquier County Deed Book 55, p. 96. (Hereafter referred to as D. B.)
3. D.B. 55, p. 96 (13 October 1855) McIlhany, Hugh Milton, *Some Virginia Families* ... (Baltimore: Genealogical Publ. Co., 1962) p. 255. A daughter, Henrietta Rogers, m. 1855, a neighbor on the west side of the Cobbler Mt., Benjamin E. Curlette of *Waverley*.
4. Randoloh Picton Rixey, *Rixey Family Genealogy*, (Lynchburg: J. P. Bell Co., 1933) (Hereafter referred to as Rixey Family Genealogy)
5. D. B. 51, p. 356.
6. ibid.
7. D. B. 49, p. 230.
8. D. B. 52, p. 149. Descendants of Nathaniel Gilmore Carter still live on this parcel and on it is a large cemetery where many of his progeny are buried. The origin of Mr. Carter remains somewhat of a mystery. In 1860 his family consisted of his wife, Mildred Jane, age 37, who listed her occupation as "weaver." She and Mr. Carter, age 45, had the following children: Mary E., 16; James F., 15; Mildred J., 13; Nathaniel W., 11; William H., 9; Hezekiah, 7; Martha A., 5; Jacqueline, 3 and Lucius S., 5 months. The road separating Mr. Carter's land was the original road through *Vermont*, known in 1852 as the Salem-Orlean road.
9. Chancery Suit #16, styled "Bowman's Exor. vs. Rixey"
10. ibid.
11. D. B. 84, p. 30.
12. Thomas Beck, "Glenara," a Beautiful Country Seat and Stock Farm, (n.p., n.d.)

13. The sulphur spring in a field near Rt. 724 still flows.
14. D. B. 82, p. 335, 22 Sept. 1891.
15. Beck, "Glenara," op. cit.
16. D. C. Clarke, Glenara in Old Virginia, (n.p., 1922?)
17. Fauquier County Minute Book 1784-86, p. 131, April Court 1785. (Hereafter M.B.)
18. D. B. 38, p. 169 and p. 277.
19. Chancery Suit #72, styled "Morehead vs. Morehead"
20. Rixey Family Genealogy
21. "Morehead vs. Morehead," op. cit.
22. Fauquier County Will Book 21, p. 308. (Hereafter W. B.)
23. D. B. 51, p. 356 (20 March 1852)
24. See "Bleak House."
25. W. B. 13, p. 64 - 4 April 1833/28 May 1833.
26. Chancery Suit #133, styled "Scott vs. Scott" (1849-1859)
27. D. B. 50, p. 380.
28. D. B. 52, p. 260.
29. D. B. 51, p. 365.
30. "Bowman's Exor. vs. Rixey," op. cit.
31. Chancery Suit #485, styled "Rixey vs. Jones"
32. D. B. 71, p. 500.
33. D. B. 195, p. 381.
34. D. B. 35, p. 325 (26 October 1835)
35. John K. Gott, "Maddux Hotels of Marshall: Lodging for 'Man or Beast'" in: *Fauquier Democrat* (Warrenton, Va.), 2 January and 9 January 1975.
36. The remains of the Maddux family, except one, were removed to the Marshall Cemetery after the Maddux family sold the farm.
37. Chancery Suit #194, styled "Maddux vs. Sanders"
38. ibid.
39. Chancery Suit #188, styled "Maddux's Admr. vs. Saunders."
40. D. B. 64, p. 278 (8 May 1872)
41. D. B. 109, p. 54 (15 July 1913)
42. D. B. 117, p. 359 (20 September 1918)
43. D. B. 125, p. 244 (2 January 1924)
44. D. B. 345, p. 160 (2 June 1977)
45. Chancery Suit #52, styled "Payne vs. Adams"
46. D. B. 44, p. 221.
47. Franz V. Recum, *Withers-America, or A. Collection of Genealogical Data Concerning the History of the Descendants in the Male Line of James Withers (1680/1 - 1746) of Stafford County, Virqinia.* (New York: 1949), p. 49.
48. D. B. 64, p. 26 (29 November 1871)
49. D. B. 81, p. 467 (25 February 1891)

50. *Free-Lance Star* (Fredericksburg, VA.), 16 April 1945.
51. D. B. 81, p. 467.
52. D. B. 81, p. 468.
53. Chancery Suit #447, styled "Jones' Gdn. vs. Jones"
54. D. B. 94, p. 69.
55. D. B. 130, p. 24 (14 February 1927)
56. D. B. 247, p. 120 (28 May 1968)
57. D. B. 49, p. 230.
58. D. B. 51, p. 353.
59. W. P. A. Inventory, "Bleak House," by Mrs. Carter Foster, 8 December 1936, unpublished manuscript, Fauquier County Public Library, Warrenton, Va.
60. D. B. 60, p. 192 and p. 194; D. B. 61, p. 359.
61. D. B. 61, p. 362 (6 June 1869)
62. Theodor-Friedrich von Stauffenberg, *The Shumate Family, A Genealogy*. (Washington, D. C.: 1964), p. ii & 185.
63. D. B. 31, p. 34.
64. D. B. 32, p. 340.
65. D. B. 39, p. 284.
66. D. B. 43, p. 399.
67. D. B. 50, p. 380; D. B. 51, p. 365; D. B. 52, p. 260.
68. D. B. 63, p. 361.
69. D. B. 59, p. 361.
70. Chancery Suit #60, styled "Smith vs. Marshall" (18361848) and Chancery Suit #70, styled "Smith vs. Spilman" (1846-1848)
71. Chancery Suit #569, styled "Gaines vs. Utterback" (1884-1933) Deposition of Kitty Gaines.
72. D. B. 131, p. 124.
73. D. B. 172, p. 52; D. B. 268, p. 60.
74. D. B. 20, p. 244 (16 August 1814)
75. D. B. 21, p. 275 (4 April 1817)
76. D. B. 39, p. 119.
77. D. B. 62, p. 416.
78. Letter from Gladys (Payne) Gartlan to John K. Gott, August 1978.
79. Brooke Payne, *The Paynes of Virginia*. 2nd ed. (Harrisonburg: C. J. Carrier Co., 1977), p. 469.
80. D. B. 73, p. 382.
81. D. B. 90, p. 136 (2 November 1897)
82. D. B. 75, p. 174 and p. 501.
83. D. B. 119, p. 95.
84. W. B. 47, p. 472; D. B. 132, p. 206 (17 October 1928)
85. D. B. 34, p. 46.
86. D. B. 42, p. 447.
87. D. B. 37, p. 135 (28 March 1837)

88. D. B. 45, p. 100.
89. D. B. 51, p. 387 (21 June 1849)
90. D. B. 51, p. 319 (17 February 1852)
91. ibid.
92. Charles P. Poland Jr., *From Frontier to Suburbia* (Marceline, Mo.: Walsworth Publ. Co., c1976), p. 230.
93. D. B. 55, p. 72.
94. Chancery Suit #485, styled "Rixey vs. Jones."
95. D. B. 60, p. 131.
96. Rixey Family Genealogy. op.cit.
97. Chancery Suit #429, styled "Foley vs. D. B. Hall's Admr."
98. D. B. 73, p. 341.
99. John Magill, *The Beverley Family of Virginia*. (Columbia, S. C.: 1956), p. 568.
100. D. B. 98, p. 294.
101. D. B. 20, p. 244.
102. Chancery Suit #4, styled "Dixon vs. Dixon." John Marshall Jr., in his deposition, "understood that he lost his life by drowning in the Potomac River."
103. D. B. 34, p. 79.
104. D. B. #3, p. 452 (2 February 1844)
105. D. B. 33, p. 336 (2 November 1832)
106. W. P. A. Inventory, "Vernon Mills," by Frances B. Foster, 6 May 1937, unpublished manuscript, Fauquier County Public Library, Warrenton, Va.
107. Chancery Suit #204, styled "James G. Smith vs. Smith" (1858-1867)
108. W. B. 21, p. 308 and Chancery Suit #72, styled "Morehead vs. Morehead."
109. "James G. Smith vs. Smith," op.cit.
110. D. B. 66, p. 30 (22 June 1874)
111. D. B. 108, p. 195 (15 May 1910)
112. D. B. 154, p. 390 (8 November 1943)
113. Will of John Marshall, dated 9 April 1832, proved 10 July 1835, with Codicils, Richmond, Virginia.
114. Letter from Mrs. John D. McCarty to John K. Gott, 7 July 1978.
115. James Keith Marshall Family Bible, photocopy from Mrs. J. D. McCarty.
116. D. B. 33, p. 379.
117. W. M. Paxton, *The Marshall Family*, (Cincinnati: R. Clarke Co., 1885)
118. D. B. 42, p. 282.
119. D. B. 45, p. 641.
120. D. B. 59, p. 836 (16 June 1866)
121. D. B. 45, p. 185.

122. D. B. 47, p. 370.
123. D. B. 53, p. 169.
124. D. B. 61, p. 324-325.
125. D. B. 55, p. 319.
126. ibid., p. 320.
127. Rosalie Noland Ball, *The Family Tree of Col. Leven Powell's Line of The Powells of Virqinia.* (n.p., 1938)
128. Paxton, op. cit., p. 53.
129. D. B. 64, p. 320.
130. D. B. 69, p. 77.
131. Chancery Suit #251, styled "Ambler vs. Brooke," (1873-1878)
132. D. B. 74, p. 147 (30 May 1883)
133. D. B. 36, p. 302 (22 August 1836)
134. D. B. 38, p. 169.
135. D. B. 90, p. 42.
136. D. B. 61, p. 16.
137. D. B. 59, p. 836.
138. D. B. 61, p. 16.
139. W. B. 47, p. 38 (7 August 1884 - 10 August 1885)
140. D. B. 90, p. 172.
141. D. B. 84, p. 520 (6 January 1894)
142. D. B. 81, p. 468 (25 February 1891)
143. Chancery Suit #445, styled "Lee vs. Lee" (1901-1902)
144. D. B. 100, p. 142 (27 November 1906)
145. D. B. 138, p. 79 (1 November 1932)
146. D. B. 110, p. 83 (30 December 1913)
147. D. B. 117, p. 445.
148. D. B. 123, p. 439 (30 September 1922)
149. "Henry L. Lee Estate, A Farm With A Reputation, Fauquier County, Virginia." (Louisville Real Estate & Development Co., 1927)
150. D. B. 130, p. 504 (18 October 1927)
151. D. B. 131, p. 282 (16 November 1927)
152. D. B. 132, p. 175 (13 October 1928)

Appendix A

Maps of the Turner Dixon Grant, 1823–1976

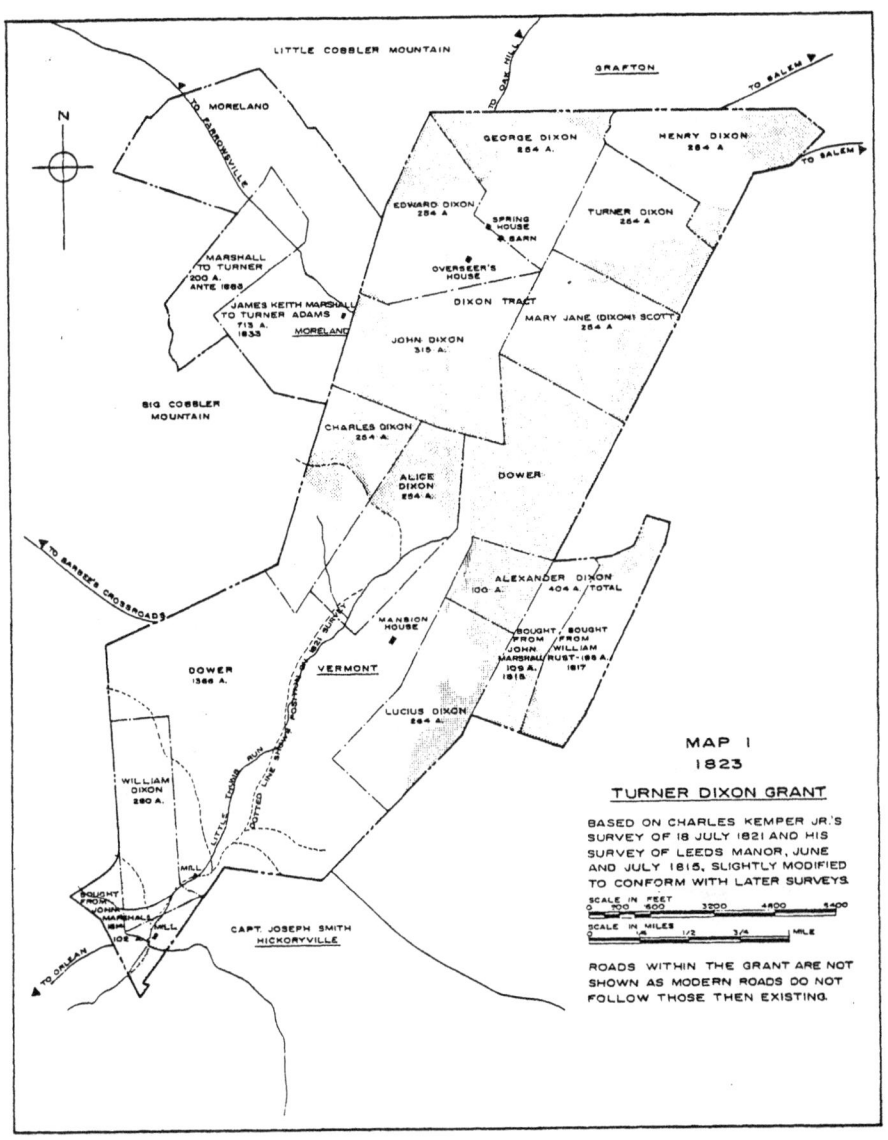

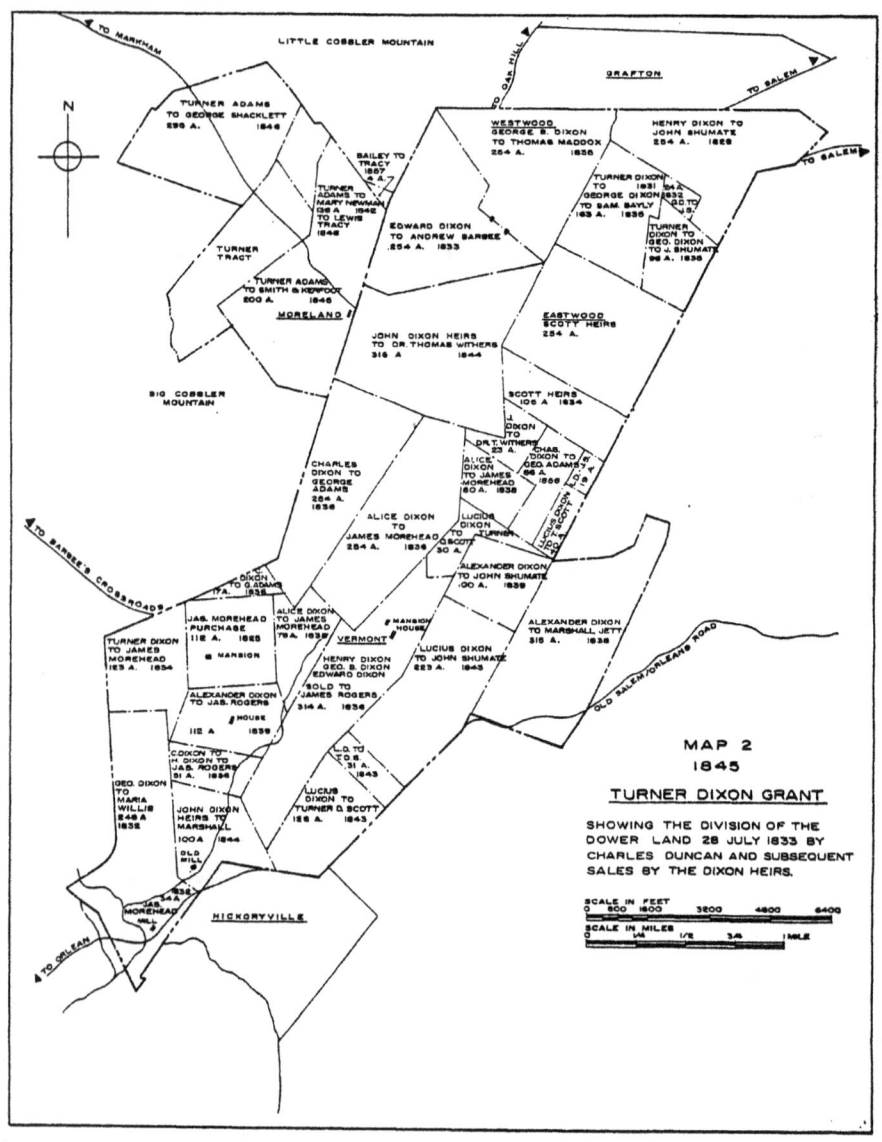

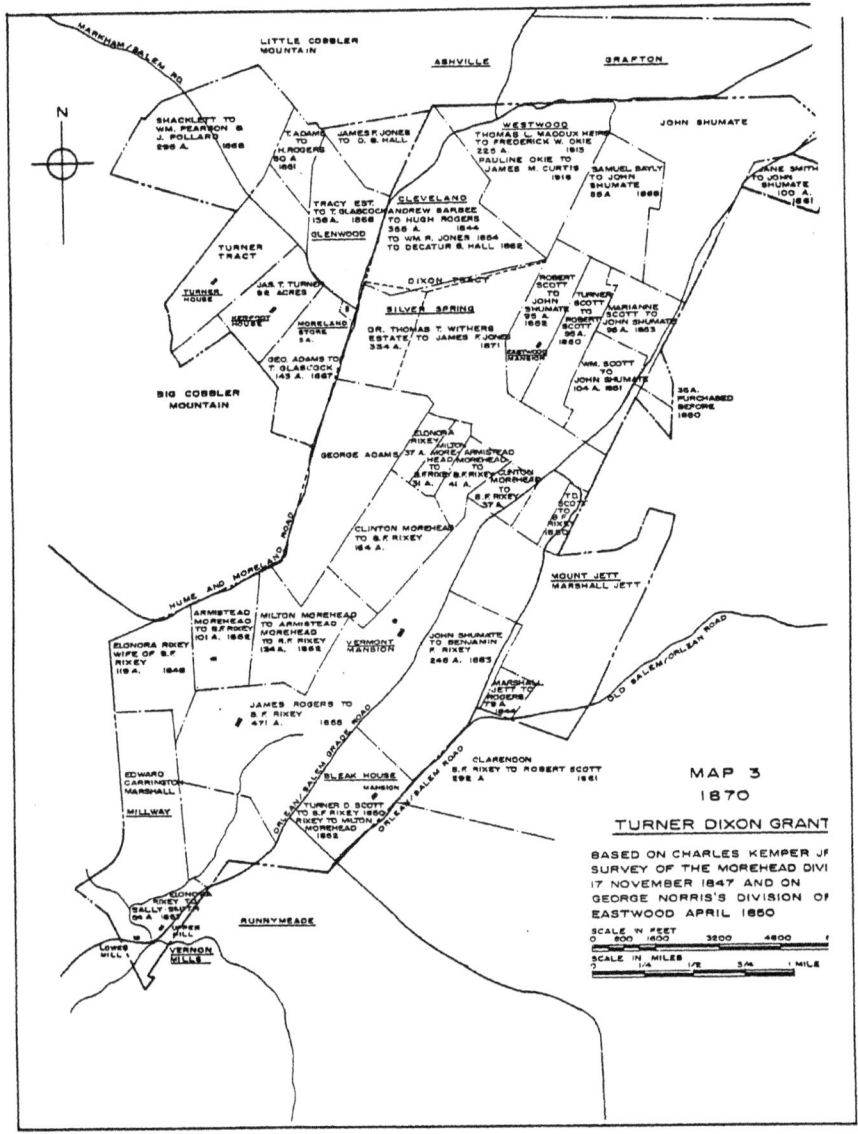

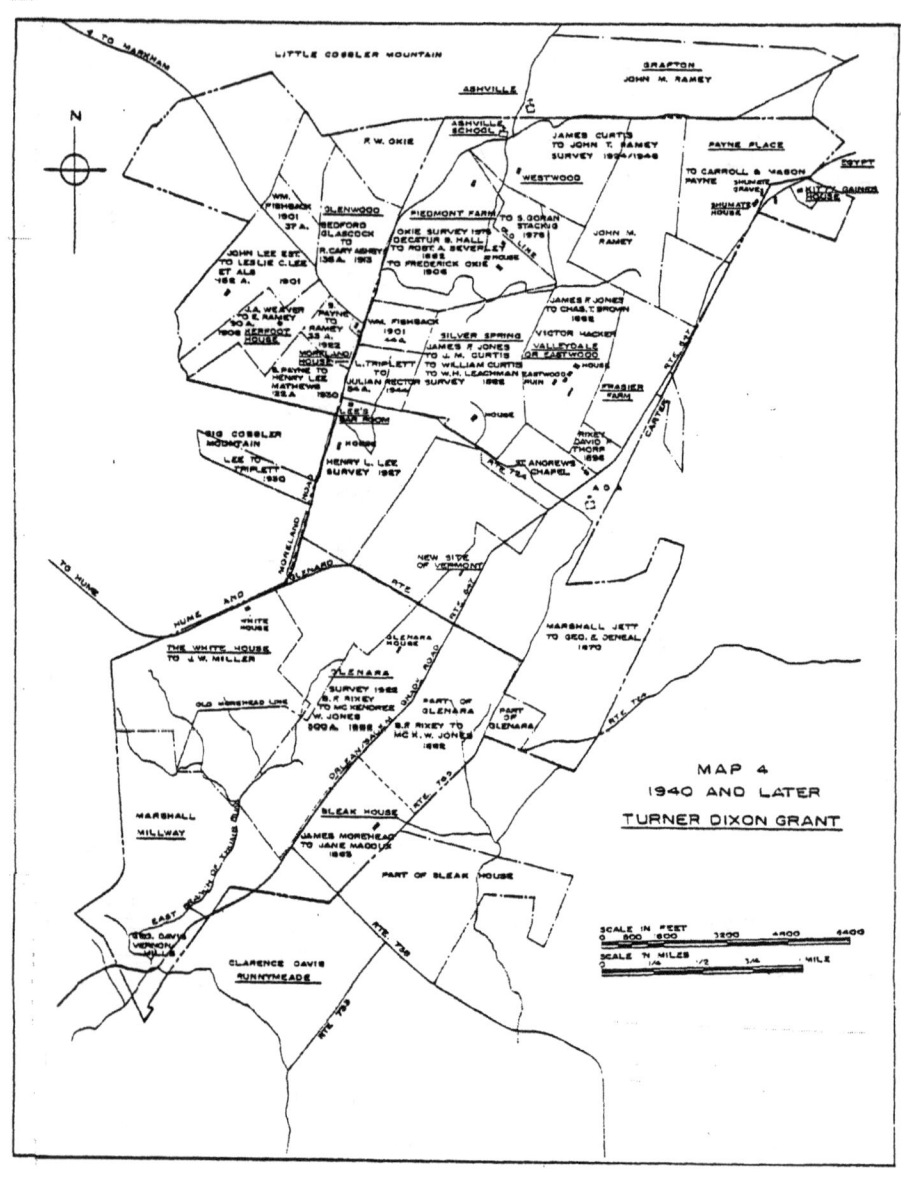

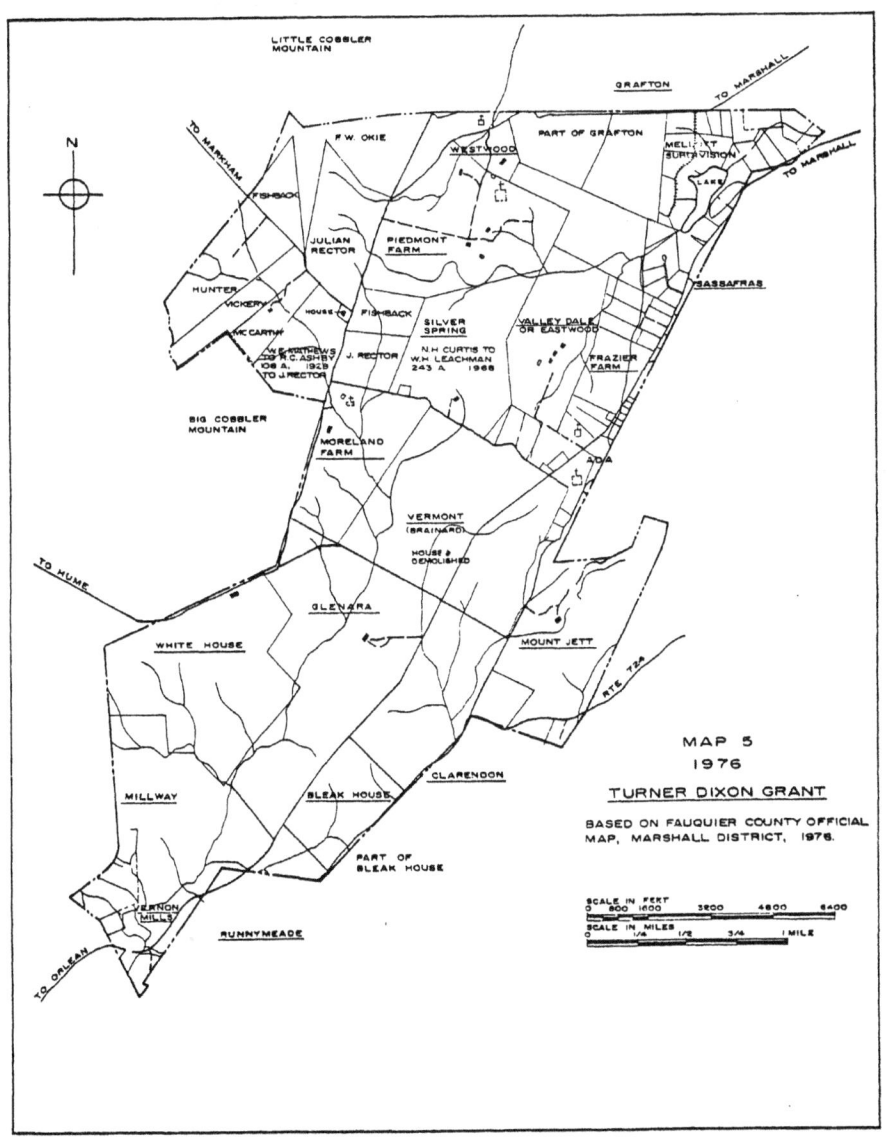

Appendix B

Life at Vermont 1810 - 1821

Lewis Payne of Fauquier County sent a letter to the *Alexandria Gazette,* dated 25 August 1879, in which he described life at *Vermont* during the time Turner Dixon lived on the vast acres, which was about 1810 to his death in 1821. He had moved his family from tidewater Virginia about this time to convert his plantation from "Dixon's Quarter" to his residence.

... Turner Dixon, a member of one of the "oldest and best families of Virginia," removed from the lower portion of this State to his plantation, called 'Vermont,' situated near Salem, in Fauquier County, many years ago, ... At the time of his removal from lower Virginia, Turner Dixon, though considering himself a broken man financially, was in fact one of the richest men in the Old Dominion. It is true that his fortune at that time had lost something of its colossal proportions, but he still owned four or five thousand acres of land, had five hundred negroes, and counted his cattle on a hundred hills. This was before the days when science had made such rapid strides in agriculture, and though the reaper and steam thresher were unknown, it was no uncommon sight to see 25 or 30 cradles running in his wheat fields. His negro quarters comprised a village, nearly a mile in extent, which was called Cherry Town. He was a fine specimen of the old Virginia gentleman, decidedly hospitable and sociable in his disposition, and wore short breeches and knee buckles, for in those days all the men of the "first families" dressed in the revolutionary or some other ridiculous style. When he gave what Virginians call a "dinner," it was sure to be an entertainment such as would bankrupt an Astor, and in accordance with the custom then among gentlemen, the "dinner" was invariably preceded by a fox chase and followed by a dance, and perhaps something else commencing likewise with a d.

This "Vermont" estate, situated in a beautiful indenture of the Blue Ridge mountains, with its broad acres rolling in broken, billowy expanse, its mansion of old English architecture, embosomed in a grove of ancestral oaks, is a place whose natural beauty and romantic attractions are softened by many tender and touching recollections. Within the portals of that old mansion joy has been unconfined those old oaken floors have often swayed with the fantastic steps of merry dancers and those moss grown walls have echoed with the light laughter of Virginia's chivalry and beauty; but now all there is silent and solemn, and will so remain, perhaps, till in future years, like history repeating itself, the sound of revelry breaks in once more, louder, clearer and wilder than before.

Appendix C

Death of Dr. T. Clay Maddux, copied from *The Baltimore American*, in the *Alexandria Gazette*, 9 November 1881 and 10 November 1881.

Dr. T. Clay Maddux, a well-known politician and physician of this city, was shot and almost instantly killed yesterday at Odenton, Anne Arundel county. According to a dispatch received last night, the shooting occurred at the Fourth district polls at the point named, and originated in one of the residents of the county being refused entrance to see the counting of the ballots by Dr. Maddux, who stood at the door of the polling room. Pistols were drawn and some dozen shots fired, one of which struck Dr. Maddux in the back. He made a motion as if to speak, but could not be understood, and expired before he could be taken into the house. It was understood last night that Dr. Maddux took down some twenty men from Baltimore to assist in the county election, one of the candidates being an intimate friend of his.

Dr. Thomas Clay Maddux was born in Fauquier county, Va., February 19, 1836, being the seventh son and twelfth child of Thomas L. Maddux, a wealthy farmer and a native of the same county. He graduated at the Alexandria Academy with distinction in 1851, matriculated at Winchester Medical College in 1857, and took his degree as Doctor of Medicine two years afterwards. While pursuing his studies he had a rencontre with Major Henry T. Dixon, of the United States Army, when shots were exchanged, Maddux receiving a bullet through his neck and lungs, which occasioned a paralysis from which he did not recover for many months. (He subsequently shot and killed Dixon in this city.) After graduating in medicine he practiced his profession for about two years at White Hall, near Winchester, and in Richmond with considerable success. At the breaking out of the war he went to South Carolina, where he was appointed a surgeon in the Southern army, and performed his first services at Fort Sumter. He afterwards returned to Virginia, where he served in the Confederate Volunteer army as surgeon to the end of the war, having been present at the battles of Bull Run, Seven Pines, and the Seven Days' battles of the Chickahominy. When the war was ended he resumed the practice of his profession in Richmond, pursuing it until the autumn of 1867, when he removed to Baltimore.

Dr. Maddux was twice married, his first wife being Miss Hill, sister of Dr. Alexander Hill, of this city, by whom he leaves one grown daughter. His second wife was a Miss Isabel Betts, of Virginia, to whom he was married in May, 1880, and by whom he also leaves one child, eight months old.

* * *

It appears that when the polls were closed a number of persons advanced to force their way into the polling room for the alleged purpose of seeing the votes counted. Dr. Maddux, who was at the window of the polling room, on the outside, objected to the entrance of anyone. So soon as he declared his purpose there were loud cries to "go for him and take him away"; "he has no business here," and similar expressions. An instant rush and melee ensued, during which two shots were fired, both of them taking effect in Dr. Maddux's left leg. He immediately left his post as sentinel and went toward an open door in the south end of the house, fighting his way through the crowd which beset him. As he turned the corner of the house a volley of shots was fired, one of them inflicting the wound of which he died a few minutes after he was lifted into the house.

When he fell his revolver was found in his hand, but his friends claim that no chamber of it was found discharged. On this point there are conflicting statements. Some say that the first shot was fired by Dr. Maddux, while other positively deny it.

The political contest which cost Dr. Maddux his life had excited bitter feeling between the contending parties interested for several weeks previous to the election, each wing doing its utmost to secure the triumph of its respective candidate for the Legislature.

Another account says: Dr. Maddux, in company with several men from Baltimore, went to Odenton on Monday in the interest of General Bond and took up their quarters in the house where the polls were held. Monday night the newcomers remained indoors altogether. The polls opened on Tuesday morning and the balloting began. Everything progressed quietly during the day, no quarrelsome signs having been shown by any one in the vicinity save by Dr. Maddux, who, it is alleged, on two different occasions had angry words with parties standing near the voting place. About fifteen minutes before the polls closed he went to the window and took up his position there, remaining until the sash was lowered and the judges within began to count the votes. During the day T. John Bowie, republican candidate for the Legislature asked that he be allowed, with Gen. Bond, to enter the room where the box was, in order to see the ballots counted, but he was not permitted to do so. After the closing of the window several of the crowd outside began to clamor for admission into the house, and insisted that they be granted that permission.

Dr. Maddux, who was still at the window at this juncture, it is alleged, exclaimed, "I'll be d---d if any one shall get in!" at the same time firing a shot, which, it is claimed, went through the coat of one Charles Hamilton, who was standing near. Maddux then started for the door on the south side of the dwelling, and when turning the northwest corner of the house fired again, the shot this time being answered by a volley from those behind. The Doctor fell near the steps leading into the house on the south end, and against the wall. He was soon afterwards carried into the parlor and died in a few minutes without speaking. It was very dark in the vicinity, and those in the crowd who fired could not be identified.

The revolver which Dr. Maddux had when found is of the old style Colt's pattern, and is the one with which he killed Henry Turner Dixon in November, 1865, in this city. This well-known feud, which, after 14 years, Dixon met his death at Maddux's hands, was, it is said, caused by the former having severely beaten an old gentleman named Phillips, who was a friend of the Maddux family. An order for the arrest of the accused was issued, but no one would undertake to execute it. Dr. Maddux, who was then about 22 years old, returned to his parents' home after having graduated at the medical school at Winchester, and on learning the state of things offered to arrest Dixon, who then lived near Rectortown, on the Manassas Gap Railroad. He sent word to Dixon that on a certain day he would visit him for the purpose of carrying out his threat. According to promise on the day specified he set out for Dixon's and had reached the house, when the proprietor appeared on the porch and fired at young Maddux, the load lodging in his neck, causing him to be under medical treatment for many months. On his recovery Dixon had left that part of the country, and the affair quieted down. About fourteen years after, in November, 1865, Dr. Maddux was stopping at the Mansion House in this city, which was then kept by Sanders & Maddux, the latter a brother of the Doctor, when one evening he was informed by his brother, Martin Maddux, that Dixon was in the hotel office. The Doctor went immediately to the office where Dixon, who was then a paymaster in the United States Army with the rank of major, was sitting in company with several army officers and citizens, and approaching him seized his whiskers, threw back his head and deliberately spat in his face, after which he ordered Dixon to defend himself, at the same time drawing a revolver. Dixon threw up his hands and said, "For God's sake Doctor, don't shoot me, I am not armed." The Doctor handed his weapon to his brother Martin, who was standing at his side, and immediately set upon Dixon, administering to him a terrible thrashing. The combatants were separated, and that night Dixon went to Washington. Ten days after he returned to Alexandria and waited at the corner of Royal and Cameron streets for the appearance of Dr. Maddux, who usually drove along that way in the afternoon with his wife. While waiting he had a talk with a gentleman who kept a tobacco store at the corner, and remarked that Maddux had not yet come along. Mr. Grigsby, knowing the enmity between the two men, closed his store and started to inform Dr. Maddux of his antagonist's presence in the city. On the way he met the Doctor, and while telling him the nature of his errand espied Dixon coming down the street. Both men fired simultaneously, Dixon's ball striking Maddux in the leg, and the latter's two shots entering his adversary's waist, so near that the wound seemed as if made only with one ball. Dixon died next morning at the City Hotel. Maddux was tried and acquitted.

* * *

Dr. Maddux's body was brought to Salem (now Marshall) and interred in the old town cemetery adjoining the Old Stone Academy and marked with a large marble stone. The monument was located by the steps of a neighboring house and removed to the Maddux family lot in the Marshall Cemetery.

Appendix D

Eastwood/Brown Farm/Valley Dale Farm

OLD STONE CHIMNEY

by

Barbara Brown Searles*

We speak of ghosts of people haunting houses, but the converse is sometimes true: there are ghosts of houses that haunt people. I count myself among these lucky haunted ones.
— Brendan Gill

    The lane into the farm, from the road to Marshall (Route 647) follows the fences, and takes a sharp dog-leg turn to the right approaching the barn and outbuildings and the farmhouse. Shortly before passing through two stone posts into the barn yard, you notice on a barren rise in a field on the right, an ancient fieldstone chimney standing alone.
    The fire which left the old chimney probably occurred about 1904-1905. As a child of five or six at the time, my father, Charles Hampton Brown, recalls the incident clearly and has often told me the story.
    In his early childhood, this site in what was then called "the little orchard" was the tenant house. It must have been a complex of several buildings, as my father has recollected and described it many times over the years. There was a two-storey clapboard house, a much older detached building used as the kitchen, a stone ice house dug into the hillside, and probably other sheds and necessary outbuildings. When a "year

---

*reprinted with permission of Barbara Brown Searles

hand" was hired, he lived here with his family. One such family that my father and Uncle Henry remembered with affection was that of Luther Canard. My father speaks of him as "a good man who went on to better things." He had a wife and small daughter. The families were congenial, may even have been related through Mrs. Canard. My grandfather, Moses Jackson Brown, who gave everyone a nickname, called Luther Canard "Cubie." However, at the time of the fire, the tenant house was occupied by a family named Gray.

My great-grandfather, Charles Thornton Brown, is said to have built the main farmhouse about 1873. Near that time, he also built, in the little orchard, near an older existing building, a tenant house which was a smaller version of the two-storey wing of the farmhouse. My father describes it as being built of nice painted clapboard with a gabled roof, two rooms downstairs and two upstairs; an entry door directly into one of the rooms with stairs to the second story. There was a chimney "up the middle."

The older, detached kitchen my father describes as looking like "the smaller part of the Lower House. It was never painted, always whitewashed." The Lower House still stands in the yard of the farmhouse, an original building, probably dating to ca. 1840. Tradition says that Charles Thornton Brown's family lived here while the farmhouse was being built.

My father speaks of two chimneys once on the site of the ruins of the tenant house. One was of brick--"that fell down years ago." I believe the brick chimney to have been the newer one for the four-room clapboard tenant house. The stone chimney remaining today on the site, I believe served the old detached kitchen. A doggerel often recited in the Brown family, of unknown origin, sheds a great deal of light on the ownership of the property, about which they might have been unaware: "Mary Jane Dixon Payne Johnson Morehead."

In the June 1880 census records, the Brown household was swelled by extra "hands" and visiting Wines cousins in addition to the resident family members. The neighboring household, that of William Lewis Hunt, his wife Sarah Catherine Brown Hunt, their infant son, Charles W. Hunt, also had a visiting 10 year old cousin, John Hampton Wines. Sarah Catherine was the second child of Charles Thornton and Mary Ann Jeffries Brown. My father and I have speculated that this young couple, just starting out, might have been living in the tenant house, that it may even have been built originally to house them.

Mr. Dick Thompson operated South Run Mill, where my grandfather usually took his corn to be ground. Mr. Thompson's daughter, Miss Cora Thompson, kept a little store (which preceded Scott Wilson's store). They were fond of my father, Charley, and sometimes invited him to come and stay for a week. He loved to go, liking the attention and the fact that Miss Cora allowed him to have as much store-candy as he wanted.

At the end of one of these visits, his father came to take him home and on the way, told him that the tenant house had burned during one night while he was away. Explaining the circumstances to a small boy, his father apparently did not go into great detail. "He charged it to carelessness," says my father. Asked if Gray, the "year hand tenant," left after the fire or whether he served out his contract, my father has a vague recollection that his family moved into the Lower House for the rest of the year. If this was summer, the farm work would have been heavy, another Year Hand difficult to hire, to make familiar with the work, the animals, the equipment and the location of things. My grandfather was a quiet, unemotional man, the opposite of Charles Thornton Brown, his father.

By the 1920s to 1940s when I visited the farm, as a child, the rubble of this long ago fire was hidden among the old orchard trees in a tangle of brush, honeysuckle and volunteer scrub that were allowed to grow up and cover it. When I was very small I recall walking up there with my father and Uncle Henry. Stock was grazed there and the hogs fattened for winter butchering. The old stone-lined pit that was the ice house had caved in, filling with leaves, the sheet tin roofing nearby among charred and scattered beams. Apparently, no effort was made to clear the rubble and rebuild. Now, all that remains is the ancient stone chimney, stark and sturdy against the horizon.

Appendix E

SLAVES OF TURNER DIXON, ESQ. as divided among his heirs in 1821.

<u>To Maria Dixon, Widow of Turner Dixon, Esq.</u>

Reuben, the waggoner
Winny & child
Sally
Andrew
William
Armistead
Harry, the Carpenter
Sally, wife of Harry
Minta
Charity
Moses
Rutha
Kitty
Lydia
Sally & child
Charlotte & child
Aggy
Billy
Nanny
Esther, a superannuate
Celia
Tulip
Young Moreton
Scytha
Gerrard
Dick
Jenny, a superannuate
Rose, wife of Dick

Sounda
Evelina
Asa
Levy
Billy, the Gardener
John
Patty
Reuben, son of Patty
Betty & cripple child
James, Coachman
Mary, wife of James
Burton
Henry
Judy
House Mariah
Esther, a superannuate
Reuben
Gerrard
Nancy & Child
Lucy
Cesar
Philip & Hannah, superannuates

To Henry Dixon:
Isaac, the cook
Jenny, wife of James & her child
Littleton
Violett
Priscilla
Jessee

To Turner Dixon:
Ben Colley
Old Molly, a superannuate
Chloe, wife of Ben
Sarah
Jane
Amelia

Peggy, a superannuate
Frank
Winny
Alice
Joe

To Mary Jane Dixon:
Dick (at Payne's)
Rose, daughter of Betty
Mary
Archy
Sally

Joe (at Payne's)
Harry
Matthew
Delphia, a superannuate

To George B. Dixon:
Lucy, a superannuate
Peter
Betty and Child
Kitty
Mimah

Sucky
Bristue
Ralph

To Edward Dixon:
Isaac, son of Isaac
Tenor
Ampy – Carpenter
Randolph

Lucy
Mary, wife to Randolph & Child
Winny

To Alex'r. B. Scott, in right of his wife, Elizabeth, Dec'd., Daughter of Turner Dixon:
Joe, called Waggoner
Joe
Sally, wife of Joe & her Child
Hannah
Sally
Moreton, the waggoner
Maria, wife of Moreton

To William Dixon:
Crawford, the Cooper
James, the Miller
Winny, a superannuate

Nanny
Mooney
Moreton, jun'r.

To Alice Dixon:
Caesar
Philip
Thomas
Mary

Betty
Matilda
Hannah

To John Dixon:
Allick
Lydia
Daniel
Nancy

Fanny, Patty's child
Fanny
Washington
Lydia

To Charles Dixon:
Anna
Polly
Peggy
Sally, child of Peggy

Philip
Burwell
Lewis
Clara

To Lucius Dixon:
Mimah
Louisa
Sally
Sam, the Miller
Scytha

Richmond, a superannuate
Caesar, jun'r.
William
Aggy, wife of Sam

To Alexander Dixon:
Sarah
Chloe
Peter
George

Peter
Judy
Robbin
Joshua

----, Henry 144 145 Robert 90
ADAMS, 105 123 Agnes 113
  Agnes Eliza 112 113 Ann 112
  Ann R 116 Ann Turner 111 116
  Anna D 111 Edward 116 Elizabeth 111 G 130 Geo 130 131
  George 37 62 64 111 116 117
  120 121 130 131 George L 119
  George Turner 112 Jane L 112
  John A 112 Littleton 116 Lucy
  112 Lucy Jane 112 Martha 116
  119 Martha T 113 Martha
  Turner 112 Mary 111 Mary
  Elizabeth Smith 111 112 Mary
  Smith 111 Mollie 111 Mrs
  Turner 112 Peter 29 36-38 40
  80 81 T 131 Turner 103 111-
  113 115 116 121 129 130
AMBLER, 126
ASHBY, R C 133 R Cary 132
  Robert Cary 121
ASHLEY, 39
ASHTON, Ann Allason 39 Arthur
  39 Henry Washington 39
  Rosina 39
ASHVILLE, 131 132
ASTOR, 135
BAILEY, 130
BALL, Burgess 7 Captain 4
  Elizabeth 7 Frances 7 Hannah
  3 James 3 4 6-8 18 James Jr 7
  James T 106 Jeduthon 7 Jesse
  7 Joseph 6 Margaret 7 Margaret P 106 William 3 8
BALLARD, Joseph 113
BARBEE, 103 Andrew 34 66 101
  102 105 112 130 131 Louisa
  102 Mrs Andrew 105
BARBER, Captain 8
BASTABLE, Gilbert M 51
BAYLEY, 91 H Clay 83 Sampson
  P 87 Samuel 33 90

BAYLY, 95 Sam 130 Samuel 94
  103 131 T Jackson 94
BECK, Thomas 60 61
BELLAIRE, 12
BETTS, Isabel 138
BEVERLEY, 125 132 Frances
  Westwood Gray 104 Julia 104
  Robert 120 Robert A 104 119
  Robert Avenel 104 William
  104
BEWDLEY, 3
BLEAK HOUSE, vii 47 51 65 84-
  87 123 124 131-133
BLOWERS, John 8 11 18
BOND, Gen 139
BOWIE, T John 139
BOWMAN, 122 123 Robert C 53
BRADFORD, George B 115 Mary
  115 Mary Brooke 116
BRAINARD, 133
BRENT, George 88
BRISTOW, Robert 88
BROOK, Edward Jr 26
BROOKE, 126 Ann Whiting 115
  Edward Jr 25 Frank 115 116
  George 115 George Jr 115
  Humphrey 115 James Vass 112
  John 115 116 Judith 115 Mary
  115 116 Rachael 115 Rachael
  Ann 115 Robert H 115
BROWN, 71 82 Annie E 32
  Charles Hampton 143 Charles
  Hampton Sr 74 Charles T 66
  Charles Thornton 66 71 72 144
  145 Charley 145 Chas T 132
  Elizabeth Matilda 25 Henry E
  73 Henry Edwin 73 John 66
  Mary Ann 66 Mary Ann Jeffries
  72 144 Mary Jane 73 Mary
  Jane Wines 68 74 Matilda
  Christie 66 Mollie 68 Moses J
  66 73 74

BROWN (continued)
  Moses Jackson 68 72 144
  Sarah Catherine 144
BROWN PLACE, 66-68
BUCHANAN, Jeffrey 97 98 Nannie
  Nannie 97 98
BURGES, Charles 7
BURGESS, 5 11 13 17 18 Charles
  ix 1-6 10 19 Elizabeth 7
  Frances Fox 7 Margaret 7 Mrs
  4 6 Mrs Charles 19
BURWELL, Claudia H 105 Claudia Hamilton 111 Nathaniel 111
CALEDON FARM, 83
CAMDEN, 12
CANARD, Cubie 144 Luther 144
  Mrs 144
CARROLL, Gray 87
CARTER, 3 Frances 6 Frances T
  31 Hezekiah 122 Jacqueline
  122 James F 122 John 6 King
  1 2 5 6 Lucius S 122 Martha A
  122 Mary E 122 Mildred J 122
  Mildred Jane 122 Nathaniel G
  51 Nathaniel Gilmore 122
  Nathaniel W 122 Priscilla 6
  Richard H 45 Robert 1 2 4 6 7
  Robin 6 William H 122
CARTER'S GROVE, 1
CAVE, Rhody 12 Thomas 12
CHESTNUT LAWN, 115
CHILTON, Samuel 80
CHINN, Janette 80
CHRISTIE, Matilda 66
CLARENDON, 114 133
CLEVELAND, 47 66 79 82 101
  103 104 113 119 131
CLINTON, De Witt 64
COBBLER MOUNTAIN FARM,
  119
COLSTON, Raleigh 111
CONWAY, Edwin 6
COROTOMAN, 1 6
COURTNEY, 41
CREECY, Carissande 45 James P
  33 James R 45
CRERCY, Cariasande 33
CURLETTE, Benjamin E 122
CURTIS, 81 J M 83 James 132
  James M 79 83 131 N H 133
  Nannie Hall 83 W N 83

CURTIS (continued)
  William 132 William N 83
DAVIS, Clarence 132 Dorcas 42
  76 79 Geo 132 George B 107
  110 George Beauregard 110
  George W 106-110 Golda 110
  Henry 60 James 60 John M 60
  John Morgan 60 Medora 110
  Mrs 60 Sally Ann Lucy 106 109
  Willis Golder 110
DAWKINS, William 1 6
DEBUTTS, D F 58
DELACHAUMETTE, Jean 88
DELASHUMAT, John 88
DENEAL, Geo E 132
DENEALE, Ada Gay 101 Ada
  Payne 101 George 101 George
  E 97 98 Ida 97 101 Lena 97
  Lizzie E 97 Martha 97 Martha
  Grant 97 Mattie 101 May 97
  Nannie 97 Nelson J 101 Susanna S 97 W D 97 William S 97
DICKINS, Charles 84
DICKSON, Turner 12
DIXON, 20 49 106 125 140 Alexander 22 26 29 33 37 40 47 90
  96 98 129 130 149 Alice 11 34
  34 54 62 120 129 130 149 Alice
  Fitzhugh 22 29 35 36 Anne
  Ashton 39 Annie 32 Annie E 32
  45 C 130 Cariasande 33
  Carissande 45 Charles 62 129
  130 149 Charles C 22 29 37 47
  84 116 120 Charles Christian
  37 Chas 130 Conisande 33
  Corissande E 33 40 E 44 45
  Edward 9-11 22 25 28 30 32-34
  45 101 112 129 130 148 Elizabeth 12 Elizabeth Matilda 13
  25 27 30 Frances 48 G B 44
  Geo 130 Geo B 130 George 25
  28 31 32 34 36 37 129 130
  George B 28-34 37 40 41 45 75
  77 91 101 102 105 109 130 148
  George Beverley 22 28 32 75
  90 102 H 130 H T 45 Harry 9
  10 11 Henry 28 29 30 33 34 37
  41 48 51 54 61 79 103 129 130
  147 Henry T 30 32-34 40 44 47
  90 137 Henry Thomas 13 16 25
  26 32 41 88

DIXON (continued)
  Henry Thomas Jr 46 Henry
    Turner 139 J 130 John 22 29 36
    80 81 112 129 130 149 John
    Edward Henry Turner 9 12 L 45
    Lucius 22 29 36-40 45 51 52
    54 65 84 90 129 130 149 Major
    43 45 Maria 13 22 25 31 33 80
    147 Maria Turner 14-16 35
    Mary B 33 Mary Jane 17 25-27
    29-32 51 65 69 75 90 129 148
    Mrs 40 41 43 Nannie 39 R 45
    Rosina 45 Rosina Ashton 39
    Sarah 9 10 Sarah Turner 10
    Turner 9-18 21 22 24-27 30-33
    35 37 38 44 48 51 52 61-63 65
    80 90 91 96 97 101 102 104 105
    109 111 116 119 120 129-133
    135 147 148 Turner Jr 30 102
    William 22 28 36 64 105 106
    129 149 William P 32
DODSON, Mary 88 Nancy 96
  Nannie Mason 96 Nannie
  Mason Shuma 96 Randolph 96
DOUTHAT, Agnes 80
DRONE, Mrs Thomas M 97
  Thomas M 97
DUKE OF NEWCASTLE, 8
DUNCAN, 62 Charles 31 130
DUVAL, Julia 104
DUVALL, L Kemp 104
EASTWOOD, vii 29 32 33 47 65-
  73 75 90 103 130-133 143
ELLZEY, Lewis 11
EVERETT, W B 99
FAIRFAX, 10 William 8
FAUNTLEROY, Elizabeth 10
  Jane 13 Thomas T 31 William
  10
FENDALL, Mary 66
FISHBACK, 133 William A 120
  Wm 132
FITZHUGH, Alice 11 Alice
  Thornton 11 John 11
FLETCHER, Joshua 29
FLOWERREE, Daniel R 33
FOLEY, 125
FOOTE, Richard 88 William 102
FOX, Frances 6 7
FRASIER, 132 133
FULTON, Jane S 97 M Mahlon 97

GAINES, Adelaide Elizabeth 91
  95 96 Catherine 91 92 94-96
  Kitty 92 94 95 124 132 Nancy
  96 Nancy Mason 91 Nannie
  Mason 95 96 Sarah Catherine
  91 94-96 Taylor 94-96 Taylor
  Scott 91 96
GATEWOOD, Eliza 96
GIBBS, Penelope 104
GILL, Brendan 143
GLASCOCK, 82 Aquilla 119
  Bedford 119 120 132 T 131
  Thomas 112 119 121
GLENARA, 23 47 56-61 120 122
  123 132 133
GLENVILLE, 22
GLENWOOD, 112 119 121 131
  132
GOOCH, 2 Governor 3 5
GORAN, 132
GORDONSDALE, 17 25
GRADY, Cariasande 33
GRAFTON, 11 18 48 48 90 94 96
  104 129-133
GRAHAM, Catesby 48
GRANT, DeNeale 101 Elizabeth
  97 Elizabeth F Nelson 97
  Herbert 101 Martha 97 Martha
  E 97 Mattie 101 President 95
  T D 97 Turner D 97 U S 93
  Ulysses S 53
GRANVILLE, 36 46
GRAY, 144 145 Frances West-
  wood 104
GREEN MEADOWS, 80
GREENVILLE, 25
GREGG, Gibson 103
GRENVILLE, 25
GRIGSBY, Mr 140
GULLIVER, Lemuel 19
HACKER, Rosa Rector 66 Victor
  66 132
HALL, D B 125 131 Decatur B
  103 104 131 132 Decatur
  Bainbridge 103 Louisa Herndon
  Love 104
HALLOWELL, Benjamin 29
HAMILTON, Charles 139
HARRISON, Benjamin 113 Burr 48
  Thomas 11 18 48
HAWLING, Martha 122 Mary 103

HAYDEN, 4
HAYWARD, Nicholas 88
HEFLEBOWER, Jacob 78 Mary 78 Mary Evaline 78 Mary Maddux 79
HICKORYVILLE, 102 130 131
HILL, Alexander 138 Miss 138
HILLY FARM, 48
HILTON, 83
HIS MAJESTY, King of England 5 7
HITCH, John 115 Mrs John 115 Rachael A 115 Rachael Ann 115
HITT, Daniel 97 Daniel Jr 97 Joanna 97 Joanna M 97
HOLMES, Brother 12
HOOE, Mary Seymour 39
HOOK, Evan Warfield 79 Kitty Lee 79
HOOMES, Col 17
HORNER, Inman 30
HUGHES, Thomas 106 109
HUME, William H 41
HUMSTON, Susannah 62
HUNT, Charles W 144 Sarah Catherine Brown 144 William Lewis 144
HUNTER, 133 Elizabeth W 64
HUNTON, Elizabeth 48 Elizabeth W 87 Eppa 53
HYSLOP, 56
JAMES II, King of England 3
JEFFRIES, George 66 Mary Ann 66 72 Sally Welch 66
JETT, Birkett 97 Jane S 97 Joanna M 97 Marshall 40 47 51 90 96-98 101 130-132 Susanna S 97
JOHNSON, Ann 48 62
JONES, 61 119 123-125 Alice P 66 103 Alice P Rixey 104 Alice Rixey 104 Anne Lewis 80 Anne Marshall 83 Col 61 Frances Barton 83 James F 83 131 132 James Fitzgerald 80 James Fitzgerald 3d 83 James Fitzgerald Jr 83 James Fitzgerald Sr 80 Jane S 80 Jeanie 83 Jeannie S 80 John T 52 66 80 103 Mary Anna 83

JONES (continued)
McKendree W 54 132 Minna 83 Mrs 54 Mrs McKendree W 56 Robert M 83 William R 66 William S 83 William Turner 66 Wm R 131
KEITH, Mary Randolph 115
KEMPER, 105 Charles 22 24 31 104 Charles Jr 25 129 131 Charles Sr 17
KERFOOT, 130 131 132 George L 112 113 George Louthan 112 Lucy 112 Lucy Adams 112 Lucy J 113 Lucy Jane 112 William H 119
KERFOOT PLACE, 119-121
KING OF ENGLAND, 7 8
KINLOCH, 29
LAKE, 133 Charles Rixey 114 Landonia 85 Ludwell Jr 114 Ludwell Sr 114
LATHAM, Shirley 99 Thomas N 52
LEACHMAN, W H 132 133 William H Jr 83
LEE, Carroll A 119 Elizabeth A 119 Estelle P 121 Henry 120 121 Henry L 120 121 126 132 Henry Lake 117 119-121 John 132 John H 83 116 118-120 Leslie C 132 Mary 120 Mrs John H 119
LEEDS, 105 111
LEWIS, Gabriel 17 Margaret 22 80
LINCOLN, 95 Abraham 41 President 93
LOMAX, Thomas 13
LORD CULPEPER, 88
LORD FAIRFAX, 3 7 8 Thomas 2 Thomas 6th 19
LORD PROPRIETOR, 5
LOUIS XIV, 88
LUNCEFORD, Mary E 101 Mason F 101 Thomas E 101 William L 101
MADDUX, 123 Alfred 79 Caroline 79 Caroline Virginia 78 Dorcas 76 78 Dorcas Davis 42 76 79 Dr 43 138-141 Edward 79 F Webb 79

MADDUX (continued)
  Franklin Webster 78 79 George W 78 79 Isabel 138 James H 79 87 Jane 132 Jane Elizabeth 78 Jane F 87 Kitty Lee 79 Margaret 78 79 Maria Louisa 76 78 Martin 140 Martin V 79 Martin van Buren 79 Mary 79 Mary Evaline 78 Mr 76 Mrs 140 T Clay 137 Thomas 75 76 130 Thomas Clay 41 42 78 79 137 Thomas L 33 42 76-78 131 137 Thomas Lawrence 75 78 79 William D 76 78
MARSHALL, 112 119-121 124 130
  Anne 83 Anne Lewis 80 Charles 12 Claudia H 105 Claudia Hamilton 111 Edward Carrington 105 109 131 Elizabeth 111 Elizabeth Matilda 25 James Edward 48 James Keith 31 62 64 105 111-113 115 116 125 129 James Markham 111 James W 93 95 95 John 17 18 22 40 80 96 104 105 111 114 125 129 John Jr 32 114 125 Judith 115 Margaret 22 Margaret Wardrop Lewis 80 Maria Willis 111 Mary Randolph Keith 115 Mrs 95 Thomas 18 22 31 80 83 111 115
MASON, Eliza Green 99 Mrs J Stevens 99
MATTHEWS, Henry Lee 132 W E 121 133
MCCARTHY, 133
MCCARTY, Agnes 55
MCCLAREN, Archibald 22
MCDONALD, Corissande E 33 40 Duncan 33 Mary B 33
MCGUIRE, Agnes Douthat 80 Jane S 80 Mary Anna Carter 83 Minna 83 Robert Lewis 80
MCKENNIE, Melissa Almira 101
MEADOW GROVE, 25
MERCER, 48 Hugh 17 John 11 Mr 18
MILAN, 41
MILLENBECK, 3
MILLER, Caroline Maddux 79 Caroline Virginia 78 J W 132

MILLER (continued)
  J William 56 Sadie 63 Wesley D 78 79 William J 63
MILLWAY, 131-133
MONKASON, ix
MORE, 131
MOREHEAD, 123 125 Ann 48 62 Armistead 64 131 Armistead H 51 62 64 65 Brother 12 Captain 64 Charles 48 Clinton 131 DeWit Clinton 51 62 64 65 Eleanora 48 49 51 56 62-65 106 Eliza F 64 Elizabeth 48 64 Elizabeth Hunton 48 Elizabeth W 87 Fany 62 Frances 62 Frances Downing 48 Frances Rixey 64 James 28 32 36 37 48 51 62-64 105 106 109 116 130 132 James Milton 51 62 64 65 87 106 Jas 130 John 48 61 62 63 Milton 52 131 Presley 48 Susannah Humston 62 William 52
MOREHEAD FARM, 54
MORELAND, 7 37 83 105 111 112 116 118-121 129 130 132 133
MOSBY, 53 John Singleton 52
MOTT, J L 56
MOTTLEY, Elise Triplett 63
MOUNT JETT, 40 47 97 101 131 133
MOUNTAIN VIEW, 51 54 61 64 65
MT JETT, 96 98
NED ADAMS PLACE, 116 119 120
NEGRO, Aunt Ruth 39 Bushrod 78 79 Daniel 12 Ellen 78 79 Ennis 78 79 Fanny 79 Frances 78 Hannah 78 79 Morten 12 Old Nace 78 79 Sylvie 12 Tulip 29 30
NELSON, Elizabeth F 97 Thomas 97
NEWMAN, John W 112 Mary 130 Mary E S 112 Mary Elizabeth Smith 112
NORRIS, Charles 131 George W 65 109
OAK HILL, 17 18 22 31 38 79 83

OAK HILL (continued)
130
OKIE, F W 132 133 Frederick 132
  Frederick W 79 104 Pauline
  131 Pauline Platt 79 104
OLD MORELAND, 121
OXIE, Frederick W 131
PAGE, George 17
PAGET, Sydney 104
PATON, John B 32 Mary Jane 32
PAYNE, 45 123 124 132 Ada 101
  Ada Gay 101 Alban Smith 46
  Alice 34 Alice Dixon 54 120
  Alice Fitzhugh Dixon 35 36
  Browning 120 121 Carroll 96
  132 Daniel 36 Daniel F 40
  Daniel Flowerree 22 Daniel
  James 115 Elizabeth Hooe
  Winter 36 Enos Withers 29
  Fannie M 96 Fannie M Payne
  96 Lewis 135 Lewis Edmonds
  43 46 Margaret 29 Mason 96
  Melissa Almira McKennie 101
  Mrs Enos Withers 29 Richard
  Cumberland 101 Richards 28
  34-36 39 Warland M 96
PAYNE PLACE, 96 132
PEARSON, William 113 120 Wm
  131
PEYTON, Chandler 25
PHILLIPS, 139
PIEDMONT FARM, 47 101 104
  132 133
PINES, 114
PLATT, Pauline 79 104
POE, Edgar Allan 44
POLLARD, J 131
POLLOCK, Golda Davis 110
  Joseph 110
POWELL, Leven 126
PRATT, Alice 12 Alice Fitzhugh
  12 John 12 13 17 John Birkett
  12 John Birkett Jr 12
PROSPECT HILL, 104
PULLER, Margaret 106
RABY, George 97 Martha 97
RAMEY, Agnes McCarty 55 Alice
  55 Charles F 55 87 E 132
  Edward 120 Edward L 121
  Eliza 96 Frances 55 Hubert F
  55 Hubert F Jr 55 Ida 55

RAMEY (continued)
  John M 96 132 John T 79 96
  Lucy 87 Norval 23
RECTOR, J 133 Julian 132 133
  Julian Winter 121 Rosa 66
REVELL, James 115
RIXEY, 82 122 123 125 132 Alice
  104 Alice P 66 103 104 B F
  114 131 132 Benjamin 48 51 52
  54 Benjamin F 23 48 51-54 56
  63-66 80 84 87 90 101 103 106
  116 131 Benjamin Franklin 49
  50 53 Eleanora 48 51 63-65
  Eleanora Morehead 49 56 Eliza
  F 645 Elizabeth 48 Elonora
  131 Fanny 56 Frances 48 62 64
  John H 80 John W Hunter 80
  John William Hunter 80 John
  William Hunton 48 Louisa
  Herndon Love 104 Molly 56
  Penelope 104 Richard 48
  Richard H 52 Richard III 104
  Richard Jr 48 Samuel 48 87
  103 Samuel Sr 66 Smith H 51
  84
ROACH, Wilfred E 99
ROBINSON, Joseph H 81
ROGERS, 51 64 Charles 32 H 131
  Hamilton 122 Henrietta 122
  Hugh 103 131 Hugh Jr 103 113
  James 32 37 38 40 47 48 101
  103 122 130 131 Jas 130
  Martha 47 48 122 Mary 103
  Mrs James 103
ROSE, Anne Allason 39 Mary
  Seymour Hooe 39 Robert 39
ROSEWELL, 1
RUNNYMEADE, 131-133
RUSSELL, John E 99 Thomas N
  96
RUST, William 22 40 96 129
SANDERS, 123 140
SASSAFRAS, 133
SAUNDERS, 123 Margaret 78
  Margaret Maddux 78 79 Silas J
  78 79 87
SCOTT, 33 38 39 44 45 123 130
  Alex'r B 148 Alexander 25
  Alexander B 25 39 51 67
  Alexander Brown 25-27 30 32
  69 Christian B 31

SCOTT (continued)
Elizabeth 148 Elizabeth Matilda 25 27 30 Frances 25 Harriet 31 John 17 Marianna 26 39 65 Marianna T 90 Marianne 131 Mary Jane 26 27 30 Mary Jane Dixon 26 29-32 51 65 69 75 90 129 R T 90 Robert 26 65 66 90 101 114 131 90 Robert E 80 Turner 131 Turner D 65 130 131 Turner Dixon 26 37 51 65 84 William 26 William D 65 William Dixon 65 90 Wm 131
SEARLES, Barbara Brown 143
SELDEN, Col 17
SELMA, 104
SHACKLETT, 120 131 Edward 26 George 130 George Washington 113 George W 113 Lucinda Smith 113 M Bettie 113 Turner D 113
SHANNON, George 97 Lena 97 Martha 97 Maurice 97
SHIELDS, William 33
SHIRLEY, 1
SHUMATE, 38 54 124 132 Adelaide Elizabeth 91 95 96 J 130 John 29 31 33 37 40 51 52 64 65 84 88-95 130 131 Mary Dodson 88 Nancy 96 Nancy Mason 91 Nannie Mason 95 96 Sarah Catherine 91 94-96 Taylor 94-96 Taylor Scott 91 96 Thomas 88
SHUMATE PLACE, 47 88 90-92 96
SILVER SPRING, vii 36 47 80-83 112 119 120 131-133
SKINNER, Benjamin F 85 87 Landonia Lake 85 Lucy 87
SLAVE, Armistead 147 Aggy 147 149 Alice 148 Allick 149 Amelia 148 Ampy 148 Andrew 147 Anna 149 Archy 148 Asa 147 Ben 148 Ben Colley 148 Betty 147-149 Billy 147 Bristue 148 Burton 147 Burwell 149 Caesar 149 Celia 147 Cesar 147 Charity 147 Charlotte 147 Chloe 148 149 Clara 149 Crawford 149 Daniel 149

SLAVE (continued)
Delphia 148 Dick 147 148 Esther 147 Evelina 147 Fanny 149 Frank 148 George 149 Gerrard 147 Hannah 147-149 Harry 147 148 Henry 147 House Mariah 147 Isaac 148 148 James 147-149 Jane 148 Jenny 147 148 Jessee 148 Joe 148 John 147 Joshua 149 Judy 147 149 Kitty 147 148 Levy 147 Lewis 149 Littleton 148 Louisa 149 Lucy 147 148 Lydia 147 149 Maria 148 Mary 147-149 Matilda 149 Matthew 148 Mimah 148 149 Minta 147 Mooney 149 Moreton 148 Moreton Jr 149 Moses 147 Nancy 147 149 Nanny 147 149 Old Molly 148 Patty 147 149 Peggy 148 149 Peter 148 149 Philip 147 149 Polly 149 Priscilla 148 Ralph 148 Randolph 148 Reuben 147 Richmond 149 Robbin 149 Rose 147 148 Rutha 147 Sally 147-149 Sam 149 Sarah 149 Scytha 147 149 Sounda 147 Sucky 148 Tenor 148 Thomas 149 Tulip 147 Violett 148 Waggoner 148 Washington 149 William 147 149 Winny 147-149 Young Moreton 147
SMITH, 92 94 95 124 130 Ann Adams 112 Ann D 113 Anna D 111 Annie 112 Burgess 7 Elizabeth 10 Elizabeth Adams 111 Elizabeth Marshall 111 James G 109 125 James Golder 106 109 James Whitacre 105 Jane 91 131 John 111 112 113 John P 106 John Puller 102 105 106 109 John Thomas 106 John Winn 105 106 109 Joseph 102 105 106 109 129 Joseph B 87 106 109 Louisa 102 Lucinda 113 Margaret P 106 Margaret Puller 106 Mary 106 111 Mollie 111 Mrs James Whitacre 105 Nicholas 10

SMITH (continued)
  Sally 105 106 109 131 Sally
  Ann Lucy 106 109 Sally Smith
  106 Sarah 105 106 Thomas 111
  Walter Anderson 97 Willis
  Golder 105-107 Willis Golder
  Jr 106
SMITH MOUNT, 10
SPILMAN, 124 John A 80
SPOTSWOOD, 2
STEPHENSON, Medora 110
STEWART, Charles B 30
SUTTON, William H 21 William
  S 21
SWANN, J B 58 John Butler 58 60
SWIFT, Dean 19
TALIAFERRO, Martha 10
TAYLOR, Charles 6 8 18
THOMPSON, Cora 145 Dick 145
THORNTON, Alice 11
THORP, David 132
TIP TOP, 41
TRACY, 130 131 Lewis 112 119 130
TRIPLETT, Elise 63 L 132
  Leonidas Lake 121 Mrs L
  Lake 63 Sadie 63
TURNER, 20 130 131 Agnes
  Adams 113 Agnes Eliza 112
  113 Ann 111 116 Elizabeth 10
  Harry 8-10 18 Hezekiah 111
  113 115 James T 112 113 115
  119 120 Jane Fauntleroy 13
  Jas T 131 Major 30 Maria 13
  16 25 35 Martha 10 113 Martha
  Adams 116 119 Martha T 112
  113 115 Martha Turner 112
  Mary 10 Sarah 9 10 Thomas 8
  9 10 13 25 26 29 William F
  112 113 115 119 Zephaniah 79
TUTHILL, Mr 61
UTTERBACK, 124

VALLEY DALE, 132 133
VALLEY DALE FARM, 66 143
VERMONT, vii 14 15 18 21-24 26
  29 30 32 33 40 41 44 47-53 55
  56 61 62 64 84 90 103 112 120
  122 129-133 135 136
VERNON MILLS, vii 47 60 104
  105-110 125 131-133
VICKERY, 133
VIOLETT, Amanda M 87 Robert
  87 Robert G 87
WALPOLE, 8 Robert 3
WALSINGHAM, 13
WALTER, F M 101 120 Frank M
  97 Ida 97 May 97
WARNER, John 3 4 8
WAVERLEY, 122
WEAVER, 120 Alpheus 119
  Elizabeth 119 Elizabeth A 119
  J A 132
WEBB, Adelaide Elizabeth 95 96
  John 94 95
WELCH, Sally 66
WESTWOOD, vii 33 41 42 47 61
  75-77 79 130-133
WEYANOKE, 22
WHITE HOUSE, 47 54 56 61-63
  121 132
WHITING, Ann 115 Frances 25
WILLIS, Henry 5 105 Maria 28 36
  105 130
WILSON, Scott 145
WINES, John Hampton 144 Mary
  Jane 74
WINTER, Elizabeth Hooe 36
WISE, 52
WITHERS, Enoch Keene 80
  James 123 Janette Chinn 80
  John 102 T 130 Thomas 130
  Thomas T 112 131 Thomas
  Thornton 80
WOODSIDE, 83
WOODWARD, L E 114

www.ingramcontent.com/pod-product-compliance
Lightning Source LLC
Chambersburg PA
CBHW062224080426
42734CB00010B/2020